John Mulgan

Journey to Oxford

John Mulgan

Journey to Oxford

Edited by
Peter Whiteford

Victoria University Press

VICTORIA UNIVERSITY PRESS
Victoria University of Wellington
PO Box 600 Wellington
victoria.ac.nz/vup

First published 2011

National Library of New Zealand Cataloguing-in-Publication Data

Mulgan, John, 1911-1945.
Journey to Oxford / John Mulgan ; edited by Peter Whiteford.
Includes bibliographical references.
ISBN 978-0-86473-819-6
1. Mulgan, John, 1911-1945—Travel—England—Oxford. 2.
New Zealanders—England—Oxford. 3. Oxford (England)—
Description and travel.
I. Whiteford, Peter (Peter C.) II. Title.
NZ823.2—dc 22 [B]

Internal design and typesetting by Ahi Text Solutions, Wellington

Printed by PrintStop, Wellington

Contents

Acknowledgements

In my edition of Mulgan's letters, which is published at about the same time as this work, I record my debt to a number of people who helped in its preparation, and I could repeat almost verbatim here the acknowledgements with which I prefaced the letters.

Once again, I am particularly grateful to Richard Mulgan for his continued support for these publications, and for granting me full access to the restricted papers in the Alexander Turnbull Library. I am also indebted to staff in the Alexander Turnbull Library for their ongoing assistance.

My debt to Vincent O'Sullivan remains as strong as it was (especially when he produced the second, unknown version of "Rustic Witness" barely a fortnight before I was to submit my finished copy). His familiarity with Mulgan's life and writings proved again very helpful, and he was always willing to engage in conversations which, while they never focussed exclusively on Mulgan, always got there in the end. Other colleagues and friends have also been helpful, and I am happy to acknowledge conversations with Robert Easting and Christine Franzen, and suggestions from Art Pomeroy.

I am, once again, very grateful to Fergus Barrowman at Victoria University Press for his enthusiastic support for this project on top of the selection of letters, and for agreeing to schedule the publication of both in time for Mulgan's centenary in December.

Finally, it gives me renewed pleasure to acknowledge the loving support I have had at home from Ben and in particular from Anne. Again, the work is so much the better for her support, and would not exist without it.

Introduction

At about noon on Saturday, October 10th, 1933, the New Zealand Shipping Company's *Ruahine* sailed out of Auckland, bound for London. She had been in service for some twenty-five years, and for the vessel and its crew the journey was no doubt an unremarkable one, but for one passenger (who confessed in a letter home to being "torn up and homesick" as the ship sailed),[1] it marked the beginning of a momentous journey to Oxford. Rather, it might be more accurate to say that the ship's departure marked the beginning of the physical journey to Oxford, for it is apparent from an earlier letter that the idea of Oxford had been in the minds of John Mulgan and his parents before he even began studying at Auckland University College. Writing to his mother in 1930, he records his surprise and disappointment at having missed out again on a scholarship to university, reflecting that having been twice on the credit list would surely scotch his future chances of a Rhodes. As events fell out, Mulgan was still nominated for a Rhodes, and there is no evidence that having been "on the credit list two years running" counted against him in any way (*A Good Mail* p. 11); but his nomination was unsuccessful, and the journey to Oxford was not financed by a generous and prestigious scholarship, but with funds borrowed by his father.

As the ship sailed north, Mulgan wrote several long letters to his parents, telling them of his life on board the vessel, his

1. See *A Good Mail* (2011), p. 17. Further quotations from the letters are identified in the body of the Introduction.

impressions of the crew and the few other passengers who shared the trip, and sharing with them some of the reading he was doing in preparation for the degree in English literature that he was about to begin. When he arrived in England he was met by his paternal uncle, Geoff, and his sister, Dorothea, who took him back with them to London briefly, then on to Oxford, to take up residence at Merton College. First impressions of London and of Oxford are also described at some length in letters to Alan and Marguerita, who must have eagerly awaited them throughout the several months that had elapsed since John's departure. Some sense of what Oxford might have meant to them may be deduced from the way in which Alan Mulgan celebrates the University and all it stands for in *Home*. He is moved by the experience of dining in Christ Church, finds almost inexpressible the charm of Merton's old quads "and the lovely library there, with its perfect timbering and air of monastic seclusion", and is equally impressed by New College, whose cloisters are "beyond praise; their suggestion of peace indescribable".[2] For John to have gained entry to Oxford, and to be at Merton with a room above one of those old quads, must have pleased his father beyond measure.

Although there are clear signs in these early letters home that Mulgan wishes to distance himself from his father's excessive and somewhat romantic view of the "ineffable charm" of the city and University, it is equally clear that it had an immediate and lasting impact on him. Within three weeks of having taken up residence, he wrote to his father promising a series of articles conveying his impressions of Oxford life: "Expect some time in February an article on 'Arrival at Oxford' & also 'An Oxford Day'" (*A Good Mail* p. 31). Whether he delivered

2. See Alan Mulgan, *Home. A Colonial's Adventure* (1930), pp. 141-49. It would be unfair to leave the suggestion that Alan Mulgan was wholly naïve in his response to Oxford; indeed, the criticism he levels at "the habit of deprecating seriousness" anticipates responses that John also voices in his letters and in several chapters of *Journey*. Moreover, the example Alan uses of disagreement over Free Trade is identical to the one John uses at the beginning of "On Meeting People".

them by February or not is not clear, but in late July, 1934, he wrote again promising "with reference to the Oxford articles, I will send you another five or six pages which would make three articles & with the photographs should make a good series" (*A Good Mail* p. 51).

Evidently, his father agreed that the material would make a good series, and the three articles were published over consecutive weeks in the *Auckland Star* under the general heading "Life at Oxford". The first of the articles was "Approach and Entry. A Colonial's Impressions" (December 1st, 1934), followed in turn by "Ceremonies of Admission. At the Bodleian" (December 8th) and "The Undergraduate's Day. Work and Play" (December 15th). The articles are all anonymous, being attributed merely to "A New Zealand Student", although one imagines the identity of the author would have been widely enough known at least in Auckland circles, given Alan's prominent connection with the *Star*. Nor did the letters and articles exhaust Mulgan's interest in Oxford, or his appetite for writing about it, and it is surely more than mere convenience or opportunism that prompts him to return to the material at intervals throughout 1934 and until the middle of 1935.

On October 9th, 1934, he wrote to his father with a suggestion that Alan might consider another book – not a novel (*Spur of Morning*, recently published by Dent, had been shepherded through the press by John, whose editorial changes caused some tension between father and son) – but a series of leisurely and sincere essays "setting down pleasantly what you think of life and politics and people and New Zealand and England" (*A Good Mail* p. 55). The effort to steer Alan away from another novel ("not literature but life", the letter concludes) is sometimes read as the younger man's judgement on the literary ability of the older. Perhaps it is that, but it is also clear that Mulgan at this time believes that the corpus of New Zealand letters needed to be bolstered by personal, reflective writing.[3] At

3. Mulgan returns to the suggestion in another letter in August, 1935.

the end of the same month, he attempts to mollify his father's concerns about *Spur of Morning*, assuring him that the Sisams liked it, and that even Bertram spoke highly of it: "Bertram told me that he thought father was certainly the leading figure in N.Z. literature which is an admission from the young. He is very anxious that more should be written and agreed with my ideas of personal N.Z. history. It is too soon to start writing reminiscences but what I am thinking of could be a chapter in them" (*A Good Mail* p. 56). In the same letter, Mulgan mentions his frequent meetings with other New Zealanders in Oxford, their reconstituting of the Hongi Club, their efforts to keep abreast of New Zealand news, and their desire to do something that would eventually contribute to New Zealand politics and literature.

Taken out of context, the reference in this letter to "what I am thinking of" may seem a little obscure, but it is clear from other letters at this time that Mulgan is at work on something of his own that involves reminiscence – just the kind of personal essay or memoir that he is encouraging his father to undertake. In the same letter in which he makes that suggestion to Alan, he confesses: "I think I will write a book next summer – I have parts of it written and thought out – about England and Oxford and myself" (*A Good Mail* p. 54). He continued working on it, and in April mentions that he has taken it with him to the country residence of Hector Bolitho, with whom he had recently agreed to collaborate on the book that was eventually published as *The Emigrants*. "I took down there the part of my own book that I have written, "Journey to Oxford". It will take me some time to finish it and of course I have no time to work at it now, but I think it is fairly good, and he seemed to take it for granted that it would be published as soon as I could finish it" (*A Good Mail* p. 74). It is the first time he has given a title to his projected work, and his evaluation of it as "fairly good" seems remarkably enthusiastic by comparison with the generally disparaging comments he makes about *Man Alone*.

However, by the end of June he has had to accept that the pressure of other work makes it impossible for him to carry on with the book. He has taken on the position at the Clarendon Press, and is committed to his work with Bolitho: "this has meant shelving my 'Journey to Oxford' for the time – another loss to art – but I shall keep it for my reminiscences" (*A Good Mail* p. 77). He does not refer directly to "Journey" again in his letters home, and there is no evidence that he went back to work on it. He is clearly kept very busy with his work at the Press, and what spare energy he has for writing is soon taken up with the series he proposes to write with Geoff Cox, "Behind the Cables". "Journey to Oxford" remained – a "loss to art" – unfinished and unpublished.

❦

"Journey to Oxford" is of interest for a number of reasons: although it can scarcely be thought of as strictly autobiographical (as examination of the contents reveals), some of it is clearly based on Mulgan's own experiences, both leaving New Zealand and arriving at Oxford, and to that extent it usefully complements material that is known from other sources, in particular his letters to Alan and Marguerita. Over and above that historical record, though, the material provides a fascinating early glimpse of some of the characters, the subject matter, the social concerns and the attitudes to land and to landscape that are to emerge with fuller expression in *Man Alone* and in the first chapters of *Report on Experience.*

Some of the correspondences with Mulgan's published work are relatively slight, and perhaps no more than coincidental – one finds here, for example, the same red tin roofs that Johnson encounters when he arrives at New Zealand in *Man Alone*, and one also encounters the same rather depressing drinking habits in hotels whose dreary sameness renders them anonymous.

Of greater significance are parallels that can be drawn with material that appears in the early chapters of *Report on*

Experience. In both texts, when Mulgan reflects on the country he has left, he is struck by its age; but particularly by the character of its age, for it is old in a way that is quite different from what he encounters in England (or later in Europe) where the places he experiences are "old with the marks of humanity".[4] Equally, one might compare the first impression he has here of London with the picture he conveys in *Report*. He reflects on the poverty he observes, and is mindful of the way that that poverty seems to him inextricably linked to the class structures that he finds so abhorrent. He acknowledges that he has known of poverty in New Zealand, but seems to find it different in character here, and experiencing that poverty while wandering at night around the streets of London seems to have been a profound shock to him. Not that his picture of London is uniformly poor and drab; there is colour in the city, the liveliness of men and women, of old Charlie the busker and the old flower girls of Piccadilly, and those images were to find another expression, not in one of his published works, but in this unpublished and untitled poem:

> A light
> flash light, torch light or neon light
> bright light from the theatre height
> a little light on the scene
> flood-light promethean, blue, red or green
> light, my old flower girl, on Piccadilly
> where we toil not, like the lily
> neither spin –
> here is sin, in God's plenty
> but oh, the brave showing
> of earth's wealth flowing
> of the flash-light, street-light and burning sign
> lipstick, paint, powder and stockings marching in line,
> on, on my children

4. The phrase occurs in *Report on Experience*, p. 36.

marching in order
it's a long journey to the border
of the promised land
but we feel the march in Piccadilly
beneath the banner of the lazy lily
the quick-step flicker of the feet
here is music moving to meet
in Piccadilly
beneath the banner of the lily.[5]

Perhaps it is the similarities with *Man Alone*, though, that most readers will find striking. In the chapter called "Rustic Witness", for example, we find a brief account of a farmer who returns from the war having lost an arm and who struggles to restore his half-cleared land that has been allowed to revert to scrub in his absence. Like Drake, in Chapter 3 of *Man Alone*, he wanders around the farm in a desultory fashion shooting at rabbits, despairingly aware that he cannot make the land pay, and unsettled by any question about another war. We hear nothing more of what happens to Drake in the novel, but in "Rustic Witness" the same character ends by taking his own life. Similarly, the two old prospectors Mulgan introduces in his chapter on London, who live in a little hut in a remote region "thirty miles away from anyone else" can be linked to old Bill Crawley. Here, they receive barely a mention, and cannot be compared with Crawley in any real sense; but the idea of a character like Crawley can clearly be linked to Mulgan's experience of these men, as it can to the "old prospector" he mentions when writing of the holiday he took with Scotch Paterson (*A Good Mail* p. 12).

The most interesting of the characters to appear in "Journey to Oxford" is the man named Johnson. In *Man Alone*, as Johnson flees New Zealand aboard the Greek tanker,

5. This untitled and undated poem exists in a single autograph copy in Mulgan's hand. It is currently in a private collection.

the *Stamboulos*, he encounters an unnamed steward who tells him of having been jilted by a girl in Auckland he had expected to marry; having previously arranged a dinner party for four, the steward orders the meal to be served as he sits alone and broods on his shabby treatment. As he tells the story to Johnson the following day, the latter commiserates with him, and advises him to forget her. An almost identical anecdote is narrated in Chapter 2 of "Journey to Oxford", except on this occasion the steward is named Johnson, and the episode of the dinner party is told to Mulgan.

Vincent O'Sullivan has commented on the appearance, in the poem "Old Wars" (published late in 1935), of a returned serviceman named Johnson who is a forerunner to the fictional figure of that name who emerges as the central character in *Man Alone*.[6] There are clearly some significant differences between the two Johnsons: the character in the poem is a New Zealander, not an Englishman, and the questioning of his war experience takes place in a desolate New Zealand farm setting, not in Brittany. To that extent, the character in the poem is closer to the unnamed old New Zealand soldier reluctant to speak of the war who appears in "Rustic Witness", and who is subsequently transformed in the novel into Drake. Nevertheless, the Johnson figures who appear in the closely contemporary works, "Old Wars" and "Journey to Oxford" provide important evidence of the development of Mulgan's central character (and of his curious fondness for the name Johnson).

Finally, this material also anticipates one of the most striking features of *Man Alone*, that of the endless struggle with the land. It has often been noted that the wars that frame the novel are only part of an all-pervasive imagery of battle; the "bit in between" (as the disillusioned Johnson characterises "peace" in the novel's introduction) is as much about warfare as anything that happens in Europe. This, too, is anticipated in "Journey", in the hard life that is mentioned in Chapter 1, as men and

6. See *Long Journey to the Border*, pp. 136-37.

women attempt to break in the land, and in the observation in "Rustic Witness" that the men "had their own fight, which was with the rimu and the rata and the matai, and then with the fern and bracken".

Not that all the images of the land are negative. Mulgan finds much to admire and love in the country that he has left, here as in *Report on Experience*. "It is at once wild and soft and the sun shines there a great deal." The peculiar combination he finds in the landscape of wildness and softness is very much of a piece with the way he describes and responds to the land in *Report*, and equally in parts of *Man Alone*. He is keenly aware of the rugged beauty of its bush and its snow-capped mountains, acknowledges the sharp clarity of its light that is so different from the softer air of England, and reveals a deep attachment to the sea that is so much part of the imagination of New Zealanders. All of this informs the first chapter in particular, the chapter in which Mulgan leaves his homeland, reflecting as he does so that "when one comes to leave such a country for the other side of the world, the parting with people and places is regarded as almost permanent, as indeed it is." As indeed it was.

Stylistically, one or two of the chapters seem rather unfinished, their prose a little pedestrian, and their subject matter somewhat lacking in imaginative force; but the majority of the book contains polished and accomplished prose, and has more interest than merely as juvenilia, or as raw material for later work. There is clearly a greater literariness in this writing than we associate with his mature style: conscious allusions to major canonical figures such as Chaucer, Pope, and Johnson; borrowings from Old English imagery and perhaps from Hopkins; and references to less significant writers such as James Elroy Flecker and G. K. Chesterton. But at the same time, his style seems already to have within it much of the straightforward and laconic prose that is typical of *Man Alone*, and that has always been assumed to derive from his reading of Hemingway.

§

Hector Bolitho was confident that "Journey to Oxford" was sure to find publication once it was finished, although that confidence may have had as much to do with his own ready access to publishers as it did to his instinctive recognition of the work's inherent merits. Nevertheless, for the reasons noted above, the book remained unfinished after Mulgan was forced to shelve it in 1935, and as a consequence has remained unpublished and largely unknown. In preparing it for publication here, on the centenary of his birth, I have brought together the material in the two separate folders described below, and I have re-ordered the first and second of the three chapters in the folder labelled "Essays". That order seems better to fit the sequence of ideas within the material, and also reflects the sense that "Day by Day" is written from the perspective of one who is no longer a student. It cannot be proven that the three "essays" were intended for inclusion in "Journey to Oxford" as Mulgan conceived it; in fact the separation into two folders and the binding together of just the first five pieces might well be thought to argue against it. On the other hand, the separation of the material into two folders and the provision of the different labels that describe them was no doubt effected when the papers were deposited in the Alexander Turnbull Library (by Gabrielle Day, in 2003). Internal evidence of content, and physical evidence of the papers, clearly show the eight pieces were all written at about the same time. Moreover, at some point when the Mulgan papers were being collected and assembled, someone believed them to be connected, and annotated the cover of "Journey" with the note "8 chapters". It is not Mulgan's hand, nor does it resemble that of his father or of Gabrielle; it may well be a note added by Paul Day, but I am unable to confirm that. Nevertheless, I believe a sufficiently strong case exists to publish all eight pieces together as *Journey to Oxford.*

The typescripts of these eight chapters are generally clean and well-preserved, and the copy is in good condition. Unlike the letters Mulgan typed, the material is relatively free from typographical error and has required little emendation. All of the typescripts contains corrections and additions. Those corrections that were effected at the time of typing (characterised by overstriking and subsequent re-typing) are not noted here; later corrections, which are almost always done by hand and inserted between lines, are recorded in the notes. Mulgan was inconsistent in his use of hyphens (and a little conservative when he did use them) and somewhat erratic in punctuation; I have regularised hyphenation, corrected occasional spelling errors, and lightly normalised his punctuation without noting my alterations.

Bibliographical Description

The typescript copies of the eight chapters here published as *Journey to Oxford* are held (with the one exception noted below) in two folders in the collection of Mulgan papers in the Alexander Turnbull Library in Wellington. Because the material has not been published before, it is appropriate to include here an abbreviated bibliographical description.

In the ATL online catalogue, MS-Papers-7906-46 bears the record title "John Mulgan – Journey to Oxford", and the note recording its scope and content reads "Contains an account of Mulgan's voyage by sea to England and his first impressions of London and Oxford". The folder contains a single item consisting of forty-six typed quarto pages and a cover page, held together with metal eyelets (although the final page is now loose). The cover page contains, in Mulgan's hand, the title "Journey to Oxford" and his name, "John Mulgan". Another hand has added, in pencil, "8 chapters" in parentheses beneath the title, and "Merton College Oxford" beneath Mulgan's name. Despite the pencilled annotation suggesting the work consists of eight chapters, only five are contained in this bound item:

> no heading; 10 pages, numbered except page 1;
>
> autograph heading "II" in ink; 12 pages, numbered except page 1;
>
> typed heading "111 LONDON"; 9 pages, numbered except page 1;

typed heading "OXFORD ARRIVAL"; 9 pages, numbered except page 1;

typed heading "EARLY DAYS"; 6 pages, numbered except page 1, page 6 numbered 7, no missing text.

An adjacent folder, MS-Papers-7906-45, has the record title "John Mulgan – Essays", and the note recording its scope and content reads "'Day by day' and 'On meeting people' describe Mulgan's impressions of Oxford and the people he met there; also 'Rustic witness - an interlude' an account of a visit to a remote country pub". Examination of the paper and type suggests that (with the exception of three pages noted below) they are contemporary with the "Journey to Oxford" material. They comprise:

typed heading "DAY BY DAY"; 12 pages, numbered except page 1;

typed heading "ON MEETING PEOPLE"; 17 pages, numbered except page 1, there is no page 11 and two pages numbered 15, without interruption of text; pages 12-14 typed on a different machine;

typed heading "RUSTIC WITNESS An Interlude"; 8 pages, numbered except page 1.

As noted, three pages of "On Meeting People" have been typed on a different machine. Among papers passed to me by Vincent O'Sullivan is a typed letter from Mulgan's Uncle Geoff, dated July 27, 1935, congratulating "Jack" on his first in the English Tripos. It appears to be typed on the same machine as these three pages, suggesting that Mulgan may have revised his text while staying at Drayton Gardens.

For all but "Rustic Witness" only a single copy of each item is extant (as far as I have discovered), but a second and quite different copy of "Rustic Witness" came to light when this book was almost ready for publication (RW2). It, too, was among papers given to me by Vincent O'Sullivan, and will in due course be placed in the Alexander Turnbull Library. Subtitled "A Study in English Life" rather than "An Interlude", and bearing a typed ascription of authorship, it seems to have been considered for separate publication, perhaps when the idea of completing "Journey to Oxford" had been shelved. All the variant readings are collated in the notes to this edition. It is not possible to reach a definitive conclusion about which is the earlier version, but in two cases, Alden/Alken and contemptibles/old contemptibles, the variant readings in the copy in the Alexander Turnbull Library (RW1) seem to be corrections, and so would imply "An Interlude" is the later, but there is not enough evidence to be sure, and the two cannot be very much removed in time. The opening sequence of RW1 suggests it is contemporary with Mulgan's visit to Alfriston in April, 1934, and the incident that forms the basis of both RW1 and RW2 is almost certainly based on Mulgan's visit to Meadle a week or so later.

Select Bibliography

Mulgan, John. "Memory". *New Zealand Best Poems of 1934.* Wellington: Harry H Tombs, [1935], pp. 40-41.

Bolitho, Hector and John Mulgan. *The Emigrants: Early Travellers to the Antipodes.* London: Selwyn and Blount, [1939].

Mulgan, John. *Man Alone.* London: Selwyn and Blount, [1939].

Mulgan, John. *Report on Experience.* London: Oxford University Press, 1947; revised edn. by Peter Whiteford. London: Frontline Books and Wellington: Victoria University Press, 2010.

❦

Birkbeck Hill, George, ed. *Boswell's Life of Johnson.* Oxford: Clarendon Press, 1887.

Chesterton, G. K. *The Collected Poems.* London: Methuen, 1950.

Flecker, James Elroy. *The Collected Poems of James Elroy Flecker.* London: Secker, 1926.

Hopkins, Gerard Manley. *The Major Works.* Ed. Catherine Phillips. Oxford: Oxford University Press, 2002.

Mulgan, Alan. *Home. A Colonial's Adventure.* London: Longmans, Green, 1930.

Mulgan, Alan. *Spur of Morning.* London: Dent, 1934.

O'Sullivan, Vincent. *Long Journey to the Border. A Life of John Mulgan.* Auckland: Penguin Books, 2003.

Phillips, Helen and Nick Havely, ed. *Chaucer's Dream Poetry.* New York: Longman, 1997.

Sherburn, George, ed. *The Correspondence of Alexander Pope.* Oxford: Clarendon Press, 1956.

Smith, David Nichol and Edward L. McAdam, ed. *The Poems of Samuel Johnson.* Oxford: Clarendon Press, 1974.

Whiteford, Peter. *A Good Mail: Letters of John Mulgan.* Selected and edited by Peter Whiteford. Wellington: Victoria University Press, 2011.

Journey to Oxford

John Mulgan

Journey to Oxford

I come from a far country in the South Seas. It is a small country where loveliness goes often unregarded. Chaucer in one of his dream poems, was led through a gateway into the "blyssful place of hertis hele, and dedly woundes cure" and there the trees had leaves that shall last for ever, fresh and green of colour, a joy to see. This one might remember of my own country, the green and unfading quality of its hills, and a traveller might come down the long gulf of islands and feel that he had reached the "well of grace, where greene and lusty May shall evere endure."[1]

Men are no happier there than in other places, except that they have little time to think; but if life should ever become an easy love-song this would be among the pleasant places of the world. It is at once wild and soft and the sun shines there a great deal. Civilisation has wasted parts of it to a bleakness of low fern hills and blackened timber, ghost trees still standing where the fire has been, but some men come to love even this. Then there are farm lands well won and held where the grass grows springingly, and where the farmers and their children work day and night to produce food which is sold overseas and is the country's wealth. At times they have been wealthy, but then they have sold their farms to poorer men, so that nearly always it has been a hard life for the men who work the land and a bitter life. Behind these farms there is land which is being broken to the same smooth state and here they run sheep and cattle in a haphazard, roughly efficient way. They have a hard life of it farming here too, although they live more splendidly; but the men become broken and old and the women worn and unthinking. None of these people belongs to a peasant class. I have known them bitter or cruel or harshly intolerant but always with something manly and strong about them and always savagely independent. They are a generation or perhaps two beyond all the wonder and despair of the pioneering days but they have gone on fighting a new and untamed country. They have had to think in some sort to live – and they work with luck into a living of wireless sets and motor cars.

In places there are long ranges of high bush hills, or snow mountains and tussock plains. These give colour to what is quiet. Everything is sharp and well-defined, no softness of mist or round hills, and the air over it all is clear and distant.

Of towns and cities it is less easy to speak. The town dwellers have been hated by the countrymen for a long time, and in many ways they are nearer to all the gods of civilisation, less direct in their ways, working for something beyond mere rest and comfort, something which they do not know and cannot hold. But close to the ugly wooden walls and the red tin roofs are the hills and the sea, so that all have something of the land near to them, and there is the same newness in what they have built as there is in the blackened trees among the fern.

Some people would call it an unthinking and a cruel country, because of its intolerance. It is not a pleasant land of song and laughter as it might be, and yet there is as much happiness there as anywhere else in the world. Nothing in it can be small and mean, and it is pleasant remembering it all now as it was pleasant living in it then.

When one comes to leave such a country for the other side of the world, the parting with people and places is regarded as almost permanent, as indeed it is. One does not see them again for many years and then, one knows, they will not be the same.

The ship in which I sailed was of about ten thousand tons built rather long and low in the water. She carried about thirty passengers, who travelled all in one class, and her holds were full of butter and frozen meat and wool. There were people as usual on the wharf to say goodbye, all in strangely animated little groups: there were streamers too and a woman was crying. The voices of the officers struck me as if I was already among strangers, for in my own country they speak the language with a more sunburnt accent that makes it quite distinctive – to some people ugly – and English of the "received standard" is the mark of foreignness or affectation. The sailors were hauling in a hawser aft, breaking the scum on the green water. It was a blustering spring day and the wind coming down over the wharves whipped up the sea in little cats' paws. The upturned faces of people on the wharf had a strange sort of pathos as the ship began to move slowly away, and farewells mean much to us there in these islands away from the world. The ship drew away more quickly and then turned slowly in the stream. The ferry boats passed her as she circled and a small launch chugged up the harbour with a very fat man sitting in the cockpit. It was no longer possible to distinguish anyone on the wharf but some of them went on waving. We began to move down the harbour and I watched from the stern the bubbles of the screw. In the bays we passed, the yachtsmen were hoisting sails and leaving their moorings for the weekend – it was Saturday at noon as I remember. Small boats and large boats, for yachting was inexpensive and the sea warm and beautiful there. A small mullet-boat, squat and ugly but good for the tideways, and with great white sails, passed close under the ship's side. Her sails hung for a moment and then, as we passed, she heeled over again and was off in a smother of spray. I thought of it as a part of my life gone, for I had known a good deal of that. I could picture them coming at evening after a hard, salt afternoon to the lee-shore and shelter of some small island, where the wind would not stir. The seagulls would come down by the shore and the bush-hens would call as it grew dark and then only our sad native owl would cry upon the night.

I walked forward again along the deserted companion way. The passengers had all gone in but as I turned by the saloon, I nearly collided with a little man in a blue suit and brown shoes. He had an amiable, weather-beaten face and very bright eyes.

"Hullo, brother," he said, "I'm looking for the bar, are you?" I was prepared to admit it.

We found it easily enough, a small room at the end of the passage almost filled by a fat pleasant looking man in a white coat, who was mixing cocktails.

"The bar open?" said my new acquaintance. "Sure" said the barman, not turning round, "It always is."

"Then beer, two beers – it's English" he said to me, "You'll like it."

We sat down on a little bench at one end of the room and raised our glasses. I was glad of something to drink and someone to talk to.

"Name is Hull," he said quickly, "Harry Hull, late of his Majesty's Navy and now on the 'igh seas." He spoke broad cockney. I told him my name.

"You been out of New Zealand before?"

"No."

"Ah, trip to the old country eh?"

"I'm going to Oxford."

There was a slight chill in the conversation and I hoped he had not been impressed, for there was little that was impressive behind me. We drank our beer while I thought of something to say. Looking out of the porthole, I could see the land slipping by, long beaches and holiday huts. The off-shore wind sent larger waves with a sharp smacking sound against the ship's side.

"Good-bye, New Zealand" said Mr Hull, suddenly and morosely, "Good-bye-ee," and then, "Did you see my wife on the wharf?" I had to apologise for not having done so.

"Ah, you wouldn't know her – I'll show you her photo some day. Good-bye, she said, and good riddance she meant. Good-bye-ee," and he beat time with his heels to the tune.[2]

The bar-man had finished mixing cocktails and stood listening to us with the benevolent interest in strangers that makes seamen so agreeable.

"You're too young to know," said Mr Hull, "but she had another man. They mostly do, don't they?" and he appealed to the barman.

"Ah, that they do," said the latter. "Most on 'em wants more than one. None on 'ems satisfied with one man."

We had some more beer and then I left them, Mr Hull swinging his legs and moodily humming "Good-bye-ee" over and over again to himself, the barman staring out the porthole. It was time for lunch but I did not want it, only sleep for I was very tired. The porthole was open in my cabin and the wind blowing in. I could hear the chop, chop and swing of the waves against the side and soon fell asleep. Someone knocked on the door in [the] afternoon, with "Tea, sir, and just passing the Barrier" but I turned over to the white wall and went on sleeping. When I finally awoke, it was getting towards sunset and the ship was moving slightly as she met the first of the ocean swell. The cabin seemed small and dark and I felt dry-mouthed and lonely. Out the porthole the sea was all alight as the sun went down behind us, and the swell was rolling rhythmically past with the land-breeze whipping the tops gently. I went up on deck and down aft to where there was a high-pooped deck, only in use when the ship was full. There I leaned on the rail to watch the last of my country.

The ship was now drawing away from the land and pointing out across the round curve of the Pacific, behind us the last of the Gulf islands with the sun shining on its high bush hills and steep cliffs, beyond that again the blue line of the land, well down in the sea. I knew that last island and had sailed round it on a still summer day, a wild fearful place with a toll of two shipwrecks, and the break of seas on it day after day. It had been very warm and peaceful then, and the sail had hardly moved with the wind, and now it all looked very wonderful and beautiful. There are few people that have seen this country that do not want to look on it again.

Another passenger joined me and we talked about New Zealand. He had not been happy there in five years, and yet I think he was sorry to see it go down over the sea's back. He said it was a good country but too small and far away. I think he wanted the stir of London where he had been born, for we all go back to our first loves and Wordsworth was right to the extent that we love what we see when we are children. "A good country," he said, "if you don't want to think." He was a schoolmaster and I expect needed clubs and cultural societies which he was not likely to find in New Zealand, save struggling in the larger towns. I felt then that there might be some things better than thought and he half agreed. He talked of some of the places he had seen in his holidays and knew that he would miss them in another country. Soon as we talked, it became dark, for there is no twilight there. The first stars came out and we could no longer see the land. Looking forward the light on the masthead swayed gently in the sky and with the wind cold about us we went down below.

We all met at dinner that night, sitting at two long tables beneath shaded and flattering lamps. When one sails by direct boat from New Zealand to England, it is still a matter of nearly six weeks travelling, with only one port of call at Panama and for the rest a wide and interminable sea to look upon. It is inevitable that with so few passengers one should see a good deal of them, as if one lived in a boarding house from which there is no escape. We were all interested in each other but rather tired and oppressed by strangers. The stewards moved quietly round on the carpeted floor, voices rose and fell, and the wide portholes opened on to a dark night.

"It's a long time since I saw England…."

"This is going to be a quiet trip …."

"I like the fish they keep on these boats. New Zealand fish are so coarse."

"I hope we have dancing …."

Most of our conversations for six weeks were like that, but it is restful being among people without ever knowing them well. Now, I heard a married man explain to the Chief Mate that he was in the Navy and was amused at his cool reception. The Mate was lean and taciturn, but always polite in society. He was more like someone in Conrad than could be believed. I heard him mention Conrad once with blasphemy as a writer of sea-stories. He condemned all writers of sea-stories and singers of sea-shanties, cursed habitually the sea and all ships, all men and most women, but I think it was only a way of speaking.

The meal was soon over and then there was coffee in the saloon above. We talked in small groups, idly and ill at ease, each conscious of his attitude to the other. Looking forward through the square windows over the lights of the forecastle, one could see the white of the waves as the ship broke them. A gramophone played loudly, and "Absence makes the heart grow fonder" we heard, "For somebody else." It amused the steward who had charge of the music: the sea-farer's ironic comment on the farewells we had seen that day. And then a curious song called "Poor me, poor you" which was sad and sentimental like most popular songs. Mr Hull caught my eye apologetically as he went out the door.[3]

Then to walk on the white, deserted deck and to watch the gleam of phosphorescent water swirling by and to feel the cool wind. When I went down along the red-carpeted passage, I passed the bar with Mr Hull already installed in it and he waved an invitation to me. But he had company already, a red-faced, small-eyed man, who was to be there a great deal during the voyage, a good little man except for his desperate and tiring wish to be drunk. I went down to my cabin which was still strewn with my clothes and luggage and all the odd things that had been left for me by those who came down to say good-bye. I put them away. It was like being in a yacht again, to have so many drawers near to one's hand. When I had got into bed, I could not sleep for a long time. Lights flickered on the seas outside and shone up on to the white deck-head above me. One could hear the noise of the water and the throb of the screw that runs through a ship. A woman's voice rose in argument along the passage and somewhere a door banged. Much later I fell asleep.

II

In New Zealand it is very difficult to read English poetry unless one has come from England or has visited it. I remember trying to be enthusiastic over John Clare beside a sea that was as blue as old wine, beneath trees that were as green as deep ice, and the falsity of turning to another man's country was hateful. There was life in the ground stronger than the printed page, so that we forgot our books and took to the seas and shores like animals.

We were in a strange position also when it came to writing poetry. I cannot truthfully explain why it was that we made the attempt but there must have been something in us that wanted to be like the rest of the world. It was all right so long as we wrote about ourselves and our loves (which were dull Swinburne) but when we turned to our native land it was almost impossible. There is a very beautiful bird called the tui[4] that lives in the deep bush and sings a song like a bell chiming. It is not a mere bird song but a man song and very rich. The tui is dark with the blackbird's sheen on its wings and a white breast that gleams on the trees in the heavy valleys. It sings one tune through the spring and another in the summer and another in the winter. I suppose most [have] wanted to write about this bird and I can hear its song now, but we were working in a strange English convention that did not know our tui and so we were beaten. The word had no literary associations for us and we were not rich enough in feeling to bear it without. So that we were left when we wrote about New Zealand – and surely no line of English poetry could contain that name

– with a kind of chill pastoral and the lines of the hills which are as sharp and clear as a charcoal drawing became blurred and picturesque. We should have given up writing poetry and made things with our hand or else told each other simple stories in prose: but there was some curse on us.

After we had voyaged five days across the sea, the sky suddenly became very blue and the sea with it. We had run into summer a month before it would come to the islands we had left. The ship did not seem to be going anywhere unless you looked at the sea-water jumping from the screw, but all round us was a half-moon of ocean and we were climbing over it and the world was round.

In the mornings and afternoons I would take a book and lie on the empty poop deck in the sun and read. When the skies became blue I chose Byron who would have seen and loved the Pacific if life had been kinder to him. When you start to read Don Juan or Childe Harold it is just like starting in a boat which you cannot direct. The wind sings and the verses clash and people talk to one another and the boat goes on. It went on and on and I did not want it to stop. There was a fresh trade wind that blew day after day from the north east and used to turn the leaves for me. In the afternoons it would strengthen and the waves would swing along the ship's side and flick up and over at the end, and you could hear the fair throb of the engines through it all.

There was a man came and talked to me about Byron one day. I think it worried him that I should be reading so old and false a romantic. He had travelled a lot and thought a great deal and he believed in poetry which I did not.

"Byron" he would say, and he would lift his hands in mock horror as he sat cross-legged beside me on the deck, "oh, the dear extravagance of old vice! and the wicked man with the soul of Cain and the cheap rant, the damned dead gossip of regency ball-rooms and the lees of a great mind."

I would try to tell him what I thought of Byron, how he saw men and women on earth and not in heaven, the greatest of realists, how he slept with the women he wrote of, and died as he said he would die; and how he put a lot of things into his verse besides bad rhymes and satire, colour and life and the sincerity of cynicism. All this is, I think, true – to me, at least; but we never agreed. I think he wanted Shelley and all the gods of mysticism somewhere beyond this bent world.[5]

There was another man who used to sit and talk to us. He read eighteenth century novels around the world and was a little proud of it as well he might be. He was a most correct, witty little man, full of gay stories about parties in London or Shanghai. He asked us what we meant by poetry and why we read it and the other man would try to tell him but I don't think it was very convincing – it never is. Poetry is just a good thing, with its own beginning and end and no meaning beyond itself. The little man would shut his book and walk away to tea, with his coat and his accent neat and correct and his conversation ready, and the other would look after him and call him a bastard colonial.

We would go down to tea also and take it with lemon to avoid the chalk-like milk. By now the few people, who were travelling so far together, knew each other well enough to wonder about the lives that lay behind each other, and you could see the three elderly women laying down their knitting at times to think[6] about it. It is difficult to disapprove wholeheartedly of scandal and gossiping for it seems such a very pleasant natural thing, to talk about other people's affairs and we all like doing it. The most interesting conversations that I had at Oxford were of this kind.

There was a girl travelling on this boat who had been married just before she left to one of the ship's officers. Nobody was supposed to know because it was a breach of company rules for her to travel in the same ship. I do not know why she had married him. She had travelled out on the same boat to join another man and had left him suddenly and was now going home again, married, but not to the right one. She used to tell us about it but it was always slightly different and always rather unreal. Sometimes on the rare occasions when they met – no-one could say what happened in the long nights – you could see them looking at one another and trying to decide why this marriage had taken place. And "Have a drink, kid," he would say, and "Thanks, Jim" she would answer and there would be another silence till the drink arrived. If they were with others, it was easier. They had not got used to being married and alone. Nobody really knew the story behind it all but what we knew was quite enough, for there are few people whom one can follow along the paths that brought them to the present and here it was enough to be interested in the slight play that we all put up to the world.

We seemed to go on a long while in this pleasant tea-party atmosphere. The days became hotter, the trade winds lessened and died away, until one night we saw the lights of Panama and in early morning we came in there on a quiet, oily sea. I have seen seas often quiet like that with the boats only swinging to the tide; this was a still hot sea with colour enough but no peace. There were some small boats, sails yellow and idle and old tramp ships anchored in the bay and up and down the coast the mist was rising in the trees and you felt that those few cool hours of the morning were worth a lot when the sun shines so close to the earth. I should like to go back some day and see it again.

We went ashore in the morning to the old town of Panama. I remember a man once telling me how he travelled in a tramcar there and how a woman opened her purse to pay the conductor and there was a live tarantula inside it. After he had said this, he thought for a long time and then said – "I wonder if she did have a tarantula – it is a long time ago and perhaps I imagined it – but it could only have happened in Panama."

There was a poor little nigger with large eyes, who drove his taxi on to the wharf as we came down the gangway; but it was against the regulations and authority in American drill and horn-rimmed glasses arrested him and gave him his ticket for the court. He wanted us to say that we called him in and he had the inevitable sick mother to support which makes tragedy into comedy, but we could not perjure ourselves and threw him and his troubles easily aside, to struggle through the coloured, smelling streets and to look at more life than most of us had seen before. It ran bare-foot alongside us, and all round us, hurrying or loitering, in old clothes and gay colours until we were tired and weary of it. Tempers are short in that sunshine for it exposes pitilessly the short-comings of northern civilisations. The women of our company came back white and ugly, the men sweating and vulgar.[7]

We could not forget all the heat for it stayed with us but we forgot most things and went sailing through the great canal until in late evening we were going down the last stretches to the open sea and the Gulf of Mexico. There was a full tropic moon and the lights of Colon were brilliant by the shore. An old negro in a bowler hat, who had shipped with a gang to work the ship through the locks, sat on the foreyard hatch and sang songs to a banjo. He sang old songs that we knew, suspect as negro songs, I imagine, about the old folks at home, and of the sun on the little cabin door, with its 'weep no more, my ladies, ah weep no more tonight', and I suppose that really he had his fat old wife in Panama and cared only for native rum, but for those few moments it was so simple and sweet and obvious that none of us laughed. And finally he too had gone with his mates on a trim little launch to the shore and we were away again.[8]

Those days amongst the islands were full of wonder. Most of us had known hot sun and red sunsets but never so much as this, with blue islands at times to watch or strange small tramp steamers disturbing the seas. We came to Curaçao, dry and ugly, with Henry Morgan's fort still standing among the cactus on the cliffs, a waterless island with oil heavy on its waters. There for a still endless morning while the ship refuelled, we could watch the fishes in the sea beside us, perhaps as brilliant as they were to the crazed mariner that shot the albatross. On shore the heat was driven back from the hills, white and deadly: some negroes worked at moving logs along the wharf, shouting together when the log moved – "w'hay, w'hay" – through the morning until it was time for us to leave again and split the brown oil on the water. We passed our last island in warm rain, a low pile of rocks with a lighthouse and some white gulls about it and then we were away for the north Atlantic.

People began to think more definitely about England as we drew nearer to it. Some of them were returning to it, as to their home country and perhaps knew it as such. They were really less interested, only anxious for the people that they would meet again, but they would tell us what we were going to see.

"You must see Brighton" said the second officer, "grand – nothing like it in the world." I think he had spent his honeymoon there and he only saw his wife once every three months.

Mr Hull was going down Brixton Rd on the first Saturday night, to the 'Palace', the pictures, the crowds and the lamp light. "There's drinks and all in the building," he told me and he would forget his lost wife for the moment. He still showed us her photograph occasionally, usually at the end of a long evening in the bar. We had become rather weary of it and less sympathetic but he was a nice little man and I think probably kinder to his wife – or to anyone – than she to him. Perhaps that was the trouble. I hope he is happy 'down Brixton Rd.' The young bride was frightened at meeting her new relatives; the Scotch brewer with the red face was looking up trains for Edinburgh; the schoolmaster, returning from exile, spoke of theatres and concerts.

For the strangers like myself it was more difficult to define feelings. We hear so much of England where I live, of sentiment, patriotic or unreal, that my own generation has reacted against it. We read English books and English papers, all our thought – even our politics – are derived from England in a rather pathetic way, and we have come to resent this dependence, less vigorously[9] than the greater Dominions, but very deeply. I think we were interested and excited, perhaps also a little shy and frightened.

It came on to blow from the west now, bitterly cold and with high seas. The sun was getting distant in the South for it was well into October. We had travelled up from where summer was just coming to the land, then under the sun in places where it was always summer and now we came suddenly to winter. The seas grew grey and the white looked ugly on them. We passed a small trawler at anchor on the banks, three hundred miles from land, her mast and funnel vanishing as she faced the rollers, a wet, wan sight, and chilling even to our comfort.

There was much drinking and saying of farewells as we drew near the end of our voyage. The ship rolled and the glasses slid down the table but we were warm and happy. In the small cabin a gramophone played and on the upper berth, the third officer made love, easily and unashamedly, to a young married woman travelling home to meet her husband. There was a detached quality in their lovemaking that implied no permanence. The purser told stories about brothels in Hamburg to those who would listen but it was enough to watch his fat sides shaking as he laughed. The first mate, urged on by long[10] whiskies and no soda, sang sea-shanties – "It's sacrilege" he said, "but you will have it." He sang them in a high shaking voice, for he had sailed on clipper ships and he knew to break the song when the pull came. Mr Hull would tell us Chaucerian stories, the winnings of war days and naval occasions, or he would sing to the gramophone and beat on the table for the steward and the drinks would go round again until they were all singing, not happily but forgetfully. They sang war-songs, as a rule, when they were together like this, 'Tipperary' and 'Keep the Home Fires Burning' and the 'Long, Long Trail'.[11] I think my own generation, or the ones who were too old for the war, are the sentimentalists. Three of these men had been in the war, but their memories of it were not unhappy: they had seen, I suppose, many things that were horrible and their friends had been killed, but none of this came back to disturb them as they sang.

Seamen are strange company. They meet so many people whom they know with a sort of careless intimacy for a short time; they have their wives and families, fondly regarded and apart from the rest of their lives; and so they go on while the rest of the world has its way, the restless pilgrims who cannot set up their tents.

A steward came in with more glasses, a small young man with smooth hair and a homely face. The purser surveyed him mistily over an empty glass.

"Have you stopped worrying about that girl, Johnson?" he said suddenly.

"Yes, sir."

"Well, put her out of your mind – she's no good."

"Yes, sir."

"She took your presents, didn't she?"

"Yes, sir."

"And turned you down?"

"Yes, sir."

"Well forget her, she's no good and you know it."

"Yes sir."

The purser turned away well satisfied. "The same again, Johnson, all round – and give the card to the mate." He wound up the gramophone thoughtfully to play the 'Londonderry Air' which was his favourite tune.[12] He did not know Ireland but was a Londoner and wise as a city sparrow.

A message came down from the bridge – they had picked up the Lizard Light. We struggled along the passage, lurching with the ship and up the wide stairway. The heavy doors blew back in our faces with a cold wind, but we went out on deck and saw the light flash twice before being driven in by the gale, and then we rejoined the purser who was playing the 'Londonderry Air' over again, humming it quietly to himself. He had seen the Lizard Light before.

Going to bed that night I met the steward Johnson watching the empty bar. He was lonely and tired for they worked long hours. "No sir," he said, "I don't much want to see England again". He was another man who had left his heart in New Zealand. "I knew nothing about it, sir, till the day before we sailed, then just a note to the ship, just a note that's all. I rang up but she'd gone out. I went up to the hotel and I'd ordered dinner for four – her and two friends. Send it in, I said to the waiter, this is all there is. I drank a lot sir, then I rode round in a taxi, I don't remember coming back to the ship."

"What did she say in her letter?"

"Just that she couldn't see me again, sir, that's all." After that we talked about places he had seen, about England and Chester where he came from, until it was time for him to close the bar and for us both to go our ways to bed.

By morning we were in the quieter waters of the channel. The wind had gone round to the east and blew coldly off the land which was hidden in mist and rain. We came into the channel traffic and began to pass the tramp ships of the world with decks that looked colder than ours. Sometimes we saw the land but never clearly and so on all day, with the fog-horn sounding at times and the restless feeling that ends every voyage. Late that night we stopped for our pilot at Dover and the next day at day-break, we were coming up the Thames.

It was quieter now. The wind had gone but over all was a greyness that was deep and heavy. I have always loved estuaries and tideways, particularly those of my own country where the rivers widen out to long shallows and innumerable channels among the mangroves, where the mud-flats lie bare and heavy with shellfish at ebb tide. This was a tideway more old and desolate than anything I had seen, old ships and barges rotting by the banks, old brick buildings and dark chimneys, and in the desolation of flat fens that lay beyond, old houses lonely and hard to come to. The sun was a stranger to these skies, as I had never known it, red, but far down in the south and hidden by the mist. As we went on, the buildings grew in upon us and the river narrowed; the ship lost way and the dark tugs took her by the head. London engulfed us.

III

London

A man might talk and write for a long time before he had explained all that he thought and felt about London. Johnson, wisest of men, wrote a poem to it which is little about London and mostly of the sadness of life. In later years he used to say that the man who is tired of London is tired of life,[13] and that too is possible, but did he not grow rather weary of life himself? And there are people who live there, the natives, the acclimatised, who claim to love it and to praise its dark ugliness. All this is possible for men love many and strange things, and there is no place to which London can be compared. For the stranger there will be only regret if he feels none of this.

There is a part of New Zealand that has never been properly reclaimed to men, the 'Erewhon' country where the mountains and the sea nearly meet. Between them there is a narrow strip of country which is all bush hills, and valleys and swift mountain rivers that are wide and difficult to cross. I remember once going into a part of this in the late summer. We left one valley in the east with its little dairy farms and standing bush and went up into the hills, across a kind of tussock plain that was swept by wet clouds and rain. We were north of the real mountains but this desert was high and cold enough. On the second day we came to the edge of the plain and into high bush again, and below us we saw a river, brown and ugly. We followed it down to the sea where it ran out into the Tasman over a bar piled high with driftwood. There was a little hut there, sheltered behind trees from the roar of the surf and the river, and two men lived in it, prospecting for gold. They were thirty miles away from anyone else and no-one ever came because of the rivers that were always flooding. Their stores had been held up by the big rains and they were living on eels that they caught in the river, big fish-like tunas, and the pith of nikau palms. One of them was an old man who had spent most of his life in such places, but the other was interesting to us because he came from London. He did not say what he thought of the contrast. They had been there some months and did not talk at all except to swear when something went wrong. But only one thing he said when we spoke of going to England some day and he shook his head and muttered that London was a lonely place. I expect that there was a story behind it because he did not think his remark at all laughable, or perhaps he had given up thinking of one thing in terms of another.

But London is deeply and basically a lonely place. It has always seemed so to me even when I have been happy there, and the reason for it must lie in the necessary impersonality of so many people living together. People have spoken of other large cities like New York which I have never seen, as being warmer and more friendly, but I doubt if it is possible. There is an exciting feeling at being in so big a place where the individual does not count, especially when one has always lived in much smaller towns which were full of acquaintances; but it wears off and leaves a cold feeling. A man once talked to me in a tube in London but I think he was a little mad. It was the morning of the Boat Race and he thought that Oxford would win. He had an infallible system by which O stood for nothing, X for ten, for for forty and D for five hundred, which proved his point. When I got up to go he began to talk to the man on the opposite seat so that I had reluctantly to discount his testimony. The English are not unfriendly, but very kind and only a little shy; and here they are driven to ignore the people about them so that there is a mask over everyone.

It was perhaps unfortunate that I should have seen the east of London first for it is not easy to forget. We have poverty in my own country of which we are ashamed enough, but it does not look like this. We drove up through miles of streets that all looked the same, and indeed were the same; and they were filled with men who were not going anywhere but were merely standing still. They all wore dark old clothes and cloth caps, flat and monotonous. It was like a great grey army which had become disorganised and lost its objective. There were children playing in the streets and they seemed happier, but they were dirty and looked cold and homeless. It was almost raining but one felt that sunshine would not help to make this more pleasant and behind it all was the dull weight of acceptance, the thought that this called comment from no-one. One gets used to this in London, used to coming out of a theatre past a man trying to sell matches in the wind and rain, used to turning from bright lights and colour in one street to barrows and old clothes in the next. It's a gay mad world to live in with fine clothes and cars to look at and cold streets to stand on, but it must take the heart out of a lot of people. It is easy enough to be sentimentally sympathetic to social evils and none of us as individuals will do anything to correct it, but I do not know which is worse, to be cynically ignorant of what is before one's eyes, or to weep false tears for the poor. And one of these two things one must do in London. I think I have resented most the people who can class the poverty and the hopelessness of this city with its charms, asking drabness as a background for colour, people who have developed the comfortable belief that all beggars have large bank accounts and that the old flower girls of Piccadilly would be unhappy anywhere else.

But one's heart beats quicker there all the same, it's a gallant circus and the reasons for it do not always matter, only the sight and the light and the life of it. I wandered round Piccadilly for a long time on the first night I was there; and it was pleasant to see so many people moving and awake, moving somewhere it did not seem to matter where, with neon and theatre light, paint powder, patches and swift feet, uniformed commissionaires and the glitter of revolving doors, and only the maestro wanting to crack his whip and we could all dance to the one tune.

But I left it at last for warmth and comfort which I found deep in the bowels of the earth, where a trim man served drinks and sandwiches behind a bar. The room was empty so that he had time to talk and he had a happy smile which must have been good for business.

"Winter again, eh?" he said and laughed. Winter meant nothing to him. I told him that it was the first real winter I had seen.

"Stranger eh? Australian?"

It was a good guess but I corrected him.

"Ah, New Zealand now, had a brother went there – yes" – and he dodged back to deal with an order. "Yes, sir – haven't heard from him for two years – guess he's all right though – never did write much."

The counter became busy and he was diverted. A young man came in and sat down on the stool beside me. He was more elegant than anything human that I had ever seen, and he looked elegantly and beautifully sad, with the charm of roses and old china. He drank some cherry brandy languidly and charmingly, then rose and walked as gracefully out. I had rather he had stayed for no-one had ever dressed or walked like that in the land where I came from.

The glory had departed and so I left also and walked into quieter streets. A wind had sprung up again and the wind does strange things in London. If it comes out of the east, cold and refreshing, you can feel it is in the south counties, in Suffolk where the churches and quiet streams are, or in Essex where they build brick houses and clay roads, but in London it is like a lost soul. You can catch it sometimes curling uneasily round the high buildings on a corner, or whipping down some long valley of a street; but it is only half the wind it was, bereft of its individuality, more London than anything. There is another wind which is all London, the hot breezes of tube stations, that play round day and night, full of the roar of hurrying trains and people, but this wind ends where the streets and open air begin.

As I walked I passed a theatre queue, and there was a little old man entertaining them. He was tearing clever patterns in paper and as he worked with his fingers he talked and sang. "I'm Charlie," he said, "old Charlie, they call me, and I'm happy here, ladies and gentlemen, singing me song, been here twenty years I have, ladies and gentlemen, singing me song". It was a brave show, but two men passed him going into a public house behind where he stood; he looked at them enquiringly to see if there was any hope of pennies for him and for the moment all the weary craft of his twenty years was in his eyes. They went in and he turned back to the queue, "Just singing me song, ladies and gentlemen, old Charlie they call me, just singing me song ..."

After I had walked for some time I came to the doors of a little public house which looked warm and inviting. England's chief glory is not her empire but her public houses. Enough – but not too much – has been written about the little country inns. There remains more to be said for the little houses of the towns. In my own country we have rather drinking saloons than inns, places with long bars and not much comfort. They are usually called the "Commercial" or the "Grand" or the "Central" which is typical enough and always seemed right to me, but we have a bad system there by which they are open all day and close at six o'clock in the evening. The men come in from work and drink thirstily and too quickly, until at six o'clock they are turned out and the streets are filled with unhappily drunken men. You can get drinks afterwards easily enough but it needs money and good clothes – both unnecessary to fellowship. Now and again, you will find some little place where the inn-keeper has known English ways where they draw beer preciously and treat you as a friend, but the tradition is against it.

In all good London streets there are public houses that are clubs and homes, where you can be known and welcomed, drink your pint or two of an evening and go quietly home; and here drunkenness is a bad thing.

This one was like many others. I found myself in a small compartment of it being served by a very motherly woman – at least, she looked motherly. Three men sat on one side and talked about football, two on the other talked about greyhound racing and after that about politics. I stood in the centre and fed biscuits to an affectionate collie dog who eyed me gravely all the time. It was very peaceful in there; their voices were pleasantly broad and soft. The woman behind the bar – it would be wrong to call her a barmaid – talked to one, and then another and we exchanged a few words on the wetness of winter and fondness of collie dogs for biscuits. "You eat too much, don't you, Polly?" she said, and Polly jumped up with her feet on the counter and eyed longingly the glass biscuit jar.

It was time to leave this presently also and to go back to the sweet respectability of South Kensington where I was spending the night.

It would be untrue to say that all this is what I feel about London now. It is a strange city which has changed to me every time that I have seen it, and this is only an attempt to set down something of what I felt when I first came to it. For I have known beauty in London also. There was one time in winter when it rained all day and the sky suddenly cleared at sunset, a sky all red to the west and blue to the east, when I watched the pigeons circling round the monument, with the roar of buses below and the clear air above. And again in winter looking over the housetops to Westminster by moon light, when everything was silver and silent. Or walking through the parks in summer from North London to the city, and once in summer too, I felt that London was happy. I had come down from the midlands in early morning, and it was in a restaurant near Victoria before the real heat of the day began. A waiter moved round with a duster which he would flick every now and again with a startling crack, to the amused scandal of the girl behind the desk. A waitress was sitting at a table with nothing to do, and he came behind her and put a lump of sugar down the back of her dress. She laughed and tried to throw it at him. Then a woman with two small children came in and had some tea. They were so obviously about to set out for a day's sight-seeing in London and were happily excited about it. I expect that as the long day got hotter, the children became tired and cross, the woman fretful and weary; the waitresses would be overworked and the waiter would think only of a night's rest; but for the moment it was very pleasant to see these people happy without being paid for it.

Of times in London I remember best some days when I lived in a room in the Strand. It was on rather a disreputable staircase. People would put their heads out of rooms when you went up to see if there was anyone with money about; above me was a room where two young men played a gramophone when they were in. On their door was a placard "Dum Spiro Spero"[14] and usually underneath it a note "Back in ten minutes". At night you would hear "Time, gentlemen, please" from the 'Bunch of Grapes' below, then foghorns on the river, and if it was still enough, Big Ben striking the hours. By day you came downstairs to meet the roll of buses and the stir of people hurrying by.

But most men who live in London stop thinking about it. To be happy there you need friends and some money, and then you draw yourself in behind the walls of a house in some long-fronted street, and make your life there, and London goes on, a ceaseless, enigmatic way.

Oxford Arrival

A friend to whom I have owed many kindnesses since I have been in England drove me by car to Oxford. A clean wind from the east had swept away the mists and the rain. The dark pall lifted from London and the sun shone in the south. The housetops were still wet and the roadways, and wet were the brown leaves on the trees, but there was green in the fields as we left London and went westward through the country. We passed swiftly Windsor and Henley and came to the Chilterns. These are strange little hills that I once found very friendly on a summer day, but now I was thinking only of Oxford and what I should find there. We went on through lowlands again and villages I did not know, and found the river again, and then suddenly we were in Oxford and passing under Magdalen tower. It rose up gloriously in the cold sunlight.

Term had begun and it was Sunday morning, the streets quiet and empty. It was hard to identify buildings in the street we came along. It might have been any little market town and then there were the high walls of a College, breaking the line of shops. We turned down a quieter way and came to a cobbled road and here the Colleges had closed in to shelter one another against the city. Their walls were high and of that strange dun colour that Oxford now means to me, and they were covered with savage iron spikes. My friend stopped the car. "I think this is your College," he said. We went in through the half-closed door and I had a glimpse of a bare, gravel court within, but we came out almost immediately for it was not the right College. I remember wondering – irrationally, I now know – why Colleges should not have names up over their doorways. A small brass plate would be very neat and simple? Perhaps not. We drove on and came to the right College.

The porter inside this doorway knew my name and I felt it as a friendly act. He gave one the impression of knowing rather more. He could so obviously explain anything. "Yes, your room is ready, sir. There's some mail here for you." There was indeed. When I came to look at it afterwards the letters turned out to be nearly all tradesmen's advertisements,[15] and I felt less flattered.

"Yes, you can lunch here now if you like, sir. And dinner, you can dine here, sir," to my friend.

"Do I need a gown to dine in hall tonight?" I asked him.

"No, sir, it doesn't matter tonight."

There was a pause in this staccato conversation. Then, "This is your scout, sir," he said. He was waiting in the lodge, a little red-faced man. He regarded me dubiously and I nodded to him doubtfully. Our relationship was not felt to be very secure.

We went to my room across the first quad, over the damp ground, within the grey walls. We came into the second quad and here there was grass and an air of quiet repose. I think they must have built it in serene times for it had, and still has, an untroubled look. Then up cold stairs, a great many of them. The stairs had the look of an unused hotel basement; there were brooms here and there, a bucket on one landing, dust in most places. And then my room. It looked out over the loveliest garden I have ever known but I could see nothing of that now. Only rather that the room was dark and needed the light. There was a bright fire but empty bookshelves were cheerless, the carpet was rather faded and I would need something to cover the white plaster walls. Was that all? Yes, all thank you.

"I've aired the bed, sir." We inspected the bedroom cursorily. It was like all Oxford bedrooms, a place to sleep in.

"I've got everything ready, I think, sir."

"Yes, thank you."

And "Ask me, sir, if there's anything you want to know."

"Yes."

"I shall be up again this evening before hall, sir."

"Thank you."

We left one cabin trunk, labelled vividly *via Panama*, in the centre of the room. It did not make the place more homely but it at least signalised arrival, and then we went down again and through the lodge into the street.

That afternoon we walked on Boars Hill. Bagley Wood was dark, with the rich smell of rotting leaves beside us, and when you looked down into the valley, you could see the towns of Oxford. There was a slight mist over them and the threat of rain again but they were clear and unified. Oxford from there was the old city of the past that we had not felt when we came into it. It drew together somehow behind its walls and though the houses had grown out round it and there were great gasworks in the foreground, there was an entity there undestroyed. Something of what I remember feeling in a letter that Pope wrote, when he rode up from London one day, and came over the hills to Oxford with the publisher Tonson talking vigorously to him all the time.[16]

We were with a New Zealander here who had settled in Oxford and made his life round Oxford and England. He talked about Oxford and how I would find it. "You'll like it," he said. "It's a good life. Don't work too hard – meet them and talk to them. There's only one Oxford." I heard that remark echoed a month later by an elderly clergyman in a train as we passed through Oxford, going west. He leaned against the window and gazed out across the gasworks and the slums to Tom Tower and St Mary's and said, "Ah, there's only one Oxford." And I think he went on to tell me what a fine man Dr Johnson was.

But on Boars Hill now we talked about how one lived in College and this New Zealander, perhaps through living in the reality of it, could be definite. Always before when I had talked to men about it, they had covered their descriptions with a mist of fantasy – half sentences about the river in summer-time a funny story about some old don, the world of poetry. But now I was beginning to feel that Oxford might really exist. It was very much a fact to this man certainly. When a man changes his country like that, he must make some sacrifice. He loses all the background that is mainly emotional, of the places that he grew up among – in New Zealand it is seas, mountains, dark trees and singing rivers – and he becomes tenacious of all the things of the mind that he can have here.

In the late afternoon my friend drove back to London and in the early evening I went back to my College. Bells were ringing all over Oxford, for it was Sunday evening, and they sounded clearly in the frosty air. We came by Christ Church as the deep tower clock struck six and then down among the churches and the Colleges. Oxford city with its shop fronts and crowds is always a strange contrast, often a hostile one, to the older world that lies behind it.

I found my College now without much difficulty, although I must confess that whenever I entered the gates during those first few days, I had an uneasy feeling that I might be wrong. It seemed darker than ever inside the quads and what lights there were threw heavy shadows. Dampness and age lay over it. The fire still burned in my room and I sat in the armchair and looked into it, from there to the window and the old elm trees in the garden.

"Everything all right, sir?" said the little man Harry, when he came in. He seemed more cheerful, and I found in time that this was the regular cycle of his day. The morning found him weary of life, purple rather than red in the face, with a cold eye like an oyster and no charity. He would mutter morosely and bang doors when he came in. Conversation was better by lunch time, especially if someone had given him beer, and in the evening, life was sunny. He had a friend in the buttery and they would go down to the Stag's Head together in the half hour before dinner time. Theirs was a good companionship: two old veterans of the College, with memories of pre-war claret days, a scorn of the modern tea-drinking undergraduate, a hatred of anything that was not in the true gentlemanly tradition of those easy-spending days. It is a common phase of a new Oxford for undergraduates to be terrified by their scouts. My own reaction was to be embarrassed by a servant. It is very difficult to justify oneself in being waited upon by another man; but I am afraid one soon gets not to dislike it, and we were cheered by the badness of this service. We used to sweep and dust the rooms ourselves when anyone that mattered or who would notice came to visit us.

A bell rang outside.

"Chapel, sir," said Harry, "You don't 'ave to go but you ought to go some Sunday. It's every night and morning but Sunday's the time to go."

"Why Sunday?"

"Ah, College tradition, sir, Chaplain likes gentlemen to go Sunday. Nothing compulsory, you understand me, sir, but he expects it."

"I see." A silence.

"Porter tells me you come from New Zealand, sir."

"Yes."

"Ah, long way, that is, sir. There was a man from here went out there before the war. Worked in the garden here. Killed in Palestine in the war, I believe, sir. So his brother told me. Well see you in Hall, sir, seven thirty. I'll show you where to sit."

I sat on thinking, and wondering if this room would ever become friendly; until at 7.30 it was time to go into Hall.

Dinner, I suppose, one felt should be impressive; and indeed the hall was handsome to look at, the three long tables with their benches. At the head and under the rich, red-robed portraits was high table with its heavy silverware. But all this was drowned in humanity that swarmed in and sat down and talked noisily. No food was served while we waited, and then someone banged on the table and they all rose as the dons came in to high table, and grace was read with a high-pitched English voice running fast over the syllables. A bench banged noisily to the floor and then another. It was a favourite College joke. Grace was over and dinner served; more noise than one had dreamed of, the dishes banged down before one, conversation that rose high over it all.

A man with red hair and a face like a saw-miller attracted me, perhaps because of his cultivated voice. He looked so much like the men I had known whose conversation had all been in expletives and unmusical accents. But I think they would have something in common. He was telling the table about his vacation in London.

"Know the brasserie below the Haymarket, eh? Ask for Henry the barman there and remind him of me. He'll remember me, yes, sir," and he went on to tell us why Henry should remember him. I think the reasons were adequate.

"You're tight again, Bill," said his neighbour. "What have you been doing?"

Bill told us how he had spent his Sunday. He had been having "the hell of a time." Lunch with a man in B.N.C.,[17] an American with a new drink, "gin and something" and after that the day had worn on to a sherry party and somewhere else. The conversation degenerated into personalities.

Dinner was soon over. Soup, meat and sweet followed each other with a heavy delayed rhythm, and savouries littered a table that was thinning rapidly. I escaped into the quad.

"Noon strikes on Oxford, noon on Oxford town...."[18]

The sky had clouded over again now and the stars had gone, but a half-moon was riding the clouds merrily. One by one lights came on in the rooms around and I went back to my own fire.

It was a quiet evening. As I moved round unpacking, I listened to the chimes and cutting across them the raucous music of a gramophone. Tom Tower rang out its hundred and one peals, one for each scholar. At ten the sullen Merton bells rang their last chime for the night, and over the meadows came the sweet airiness of Magdalen – shades of Oscar Wilde.

I went to bed and slept easily as one always does in Oxford town.

Early Days

I think what worried me most in those first few days at Oxford was my inability to find anything to do, or anyone who could tell me what I ought to do. When I arrived, I had a vague idea that I should call on the Head of the College and pay my respects to him.

"Good Lord, sir," said the porter thoroughly startled, "not on Sunday, sir, nor any time. The old gentleman'll send for you any time he wants you."

One man I found who was glad to see me in a direct way, the College bursar who required a large deposit of money. Then I found a senior tutor, disengaged by some accident for five minutes. He assimilated the story of my life and my hopes for the future within that time and sent me to the man who was to be charged with tutoring me, the most charming person whom I can remember meeting. He balanced himself on a chair and smoked a cigarette while we talked about the development of cricket in New Zealand. I suppose the guide books would lead one to expect inconsequentiality in Oxford but this was the more charming because it was sincere. Later, I met dons, older men who had thought about Oxford and the Oxford attitude and who had developed a way of talking about nothing to undergraduates and a manner that was exasperating for its conscious ease. But there was nothing of this here, only a sincerity for which I became very grateful as time went on, for I know that I laboured under the disadvantages of a Colonial belief that equated – not always incorrectly – personal charm with insincerity.

All this, I think, took three days. Finally I met the head of the College. They told strange stories about him, that he was over ninety, that he had not been out of his house since 1903, that he was deaf and half blind. But he sent me a quite legible note, asking me to come before him to be entered on the College books. I went and rang the bell before an ugly gargoyled house and waited coldly in the street. Nothing happened. I rang again and waited and then at last the door opened and a pale, sunless butler admitted me. I waited in the hall, dimly overhearing a loudly whispered colloquy within, and then I was shown into a vast museum-like room. He stood by the fire, looking as old as sin. Then he came forward, moving with difficulty. His face was quite expressionless. I once met a man as old as that, a gum-digger in a little hut on the edge of lost forest country, with a tobacco-stained beard and no teeth.

He shook my hand. "I want to ask you a question," he said. It was not a conversational opening. "Are you willing to obey the rules and statutes of the College, in so far as they apply to you?" he went on.

"Yes."

"Will you sign your name in this book?" I did so and turned to go. "Work hard, young man," he said – a well-calculated remark. As I went out, he was making his way painfully back to the fire. The butler showed me out on to the street.

After that, matriculation was not enlivening. The Vice-Chancellor was a young man of about seventy, rich in red robes, and his mace-bearers supplied the ceremony for which Colonials and Americans will pay dearly. "Quo die mihi comparuit…"[19] he said, as if pronouncing a mediaeval curse. He bowed stiffly and I went home by way of All Souls.

And age again in the Bodleian where, with cap and gown, I presented myself for admission as a reader. The ante-rooms were young enough but within, the grammarians were working towards their funerals. There was one old lady who fascinated me. She was white haired and saintly looking, but she had left her real place which was by a fireside with a singing kettle and an old cat, to sit day after day poring over black-letter folios. But one could come down from there to see the white pinnacles of All Souls, and, if England was kind enough, a clear sky, and one would thank God for other things than scholarship.

But there was enjoyment to be had there also, in this world that was so old and yet so new to me.

"Do you write poetry?" said a man who came in to take me out to dinner. While we went down the street, he recited some of his own.

"Like it?"

"Enormously."

We dined well. And then we went to a little club that read ripe and bawdy Restoration plays, and we drank the club toast of warm rum punch. Later we were going back along the street, while he shouted aloud another of his poems. It was a good poem, too.

And dinner with a don.

"Delighted to see you." He was too busy to stop writing. "Help yourself to sherry."

We exchanged a few perfunctory remarks about our one mutual acquaintance. Then suddenly, "know anything about birth control?" I said it was not a subject of which I had an expert knowledge. "Ah, good thing to know about," he said, "find it talked a lot about here. Don't want to feel a fool. Ask me anything you want to know."

We went to dinner. There I sat next to a delightful man who asked me what I thought of the Oxford accent. We found that we could arrive at no satisfactory definition of it, except that he spoke it and I didn't. They began talking about the War in the common room afterwards.

"I got a wire," said one middle-aged man, "saying 'will you proceed Army H.Q., rank of acting-captain,'" and he told us how he had proceeded to take charge of the manufacture of gasmasks. I had the impression that some of the company had heard the story before. Another man had been an intelligence officer in the Mediterranean. Those had been the days. A little, shy man regarded them solemnly.

"I only remember shooting at one man," he said. "I was a private, and I missed him. The corporal cursed me for a blundering fool, and the next moment they shot him through the head." He laughed with appreciative recollection, but I think that the 'officers' felt that he had lowered the standard of the common room.

But to speak truly, all that I can really call to mind of those first few weeks at Oxford, is the fire that I used to stare at, while I thought of other things, of sun and sea, and summer coming to all the people that I knew on the other side of the world. There was a little cottage there on a wooded point where I knew some of them would be, away from all roads, with the sea washing round its red rocks. On a still summer morning, the boat would swing quietly with the tide, until, as the sun rose, the sea breeze would come up the harbour, softly at first, just darkening the water, and then there would be a fair wind strengthening and it would be sailing time. By evening, when it had died again, the bush-hens would be calling from the hills and the gulls fighting on the mud-flats, and as the sun set they would come in and be lighting a drift-wood fire in the cottage.

For I was oppressed by my first contact with age and winter. Here in England, the day was stillborn in a sort of agony. A red sun came through the fog and vanished again while the mists lay heavily on the meadow trees, and then it was night again, and perhaps rain was falling. That other country had been old, but not with men. It had been old as a mountain glacier is old, worn clean by each season. Here everything seemed to speak of men long ago, and they are sad enough in the present without always remembering them in the past. The weight of old associations and of the winter they endured was too heavy, and I could only assume that people who lived here had become unconscious of them.

On Meeting People

After I had been in Oxford for a few weeks I began to lose all sense of strangeness and all sense of perspective. It was not that I could accept this new world or feel myself at home in it, but that life had to be lived there in a curiously unobservant way, in which each day became a series of unco-ordinated movements from breakfast, to lunch, to tea, to dinner, to coffee. Life was so easy there that everything came to lack emphasis. In a general way – and I think this must be true for everyone except film-stars and politicians – there is a certain amount of routine which is the background on which things stand out; so that you think of a week as centering round one incident, and you look back at your life as at a temperature chart. But in Oxford they have removed, through slow centuries, the compulsion of a routine, and even in Dr Johnson's day there was sliding in Christ Church meadows.[20]

The longer I lived in Oxford, the more I realised that one needs to be trained to belong to the leisured classes. When we were students in New Zealand, we were very apologetic about it. If we were not at lectures, which, being of a low standard, we were compelled to attend, we felt that we could only justify ourselves by a continued application to books, and even in that we blushed before the money-making merchants of the city when they cared to notice us. But we were saved by having to do this for only six months of the year, and for the rest we could sometimes make the pretence of earning our living. Most of our fellow-students worked all the time in offices and came in the evenings to our lectures. It was not a country which thought very much of leisured reflection, least of all as a pastime for[21] the young.

I found that in Oxford the pleasures of life were the pleasures of society.

"What did you do at Oxford?" they asked him.

"I talked with a lot of young men," he replied.

"And what did you talk about?" they ventured to enquire.

"About everything," he said vaguely.

It seemed to me when I first arrived that the main topics of conversation were the public school system, Oxford and women. The first they decried, the second they laughed about, and the third they sought knowledge of. But other things were at times talked about. And what worried me again was that they did not apparently expect to learn anything of each other. There had always seemed to me to be something immoral in a man's arguing a case in which he does not believe; but here conversation tended to be regarded as an art in itself. There was no intensity of argument to arrive at a conclusion. I once knew two men who stopped walking together to the train in the morning because they disagreed on the question of Free Trade. It seems improbable that either of them was an Oxford man. For the young men of Oxford dislike being forced to decide a question. They sit and eat meals together, discussing with complete and academic abandon, everything on earth.

And I found in time that this was more than a mannerism. It was an attitude to life. The men of Oxford were like this because they were completely agnostic. They did not believe in anything and they knew by experience that nothing could be believed in, and each activity of the place was an attempt to find something to which they could give credence.

I did not understand this at the time but I was occupied merely in meeting people and I found it a new and exciting form of pleasure. There was a lightness about everything which made it easy and delightful. When I think back to friends I made before, it is always in terms of action that I remember them, of incidents that happened to us and of how we reacted to them. But men I knew at Oxford live as personalities to me for the way they looked and laughed and for the things they said.

And the Englishmen who go to Oxford are very charming. I have become used to them now, so that I can almost think of some of them as being offensive – like the strange men of a dying race who have been to the best schools and cannot forget it, or the little men who have made reputations at Oxford in some way, and seem to have conquered the world. But it is a mental attitude that I find offensive, and familiarity has bred a contempt that is probably mutual. To strangers they would always be charming.

It was this ease of manner on meeting people casually that so surprised me. In New Zealand we had not been taught that, only a little elementary grammar to help us if there was anything that particularly needed saying. People who spoke well – at least, among the young – were usually distrusted. We venerated the strong, silent men who played football boldly, drank their beer well, and said nothing. I have sometimes wondered since, if some of these Olympians can possibly have suffered from shyness, but it is an act of impiety to say this against my country's gods.

There was a man at the University College[22] there whom I knew well. He came in from a farm in the country for some education, because he wanted to go in for politics. It was a new approach. New Zealand's successful politicians have been countrymen, and they love to tell stories of how this one debated questions of land tax on top of a haystack and how another received dispatches while he sheared his sheep. This friend of mine was going to walk the same road with the added prestige of education. He was rugged and huge, with hair on his chest and he used to wear a bowler hat and carry an umbrella. Nobody laughed at him because he became heavyweight champion of the University. But he could not or would not pass his examinations and so he went back to his farm, despising all things academic and demanding "plain men who will face the facts". He will probably be a very successful politician, nevertheless. When I last met him, I was in a car and he was driving an old buggy along a country road. The harness was done up with string and he was wearing old dungarees, a torn shirt and a buttonless waistcoat that flapped in the wind. He knew that I was going to Oxford and he stopped to say good-bye.

"Don't get soft, boy," he said. "If you get there with those fellows and start dressing up and talking fancy, I'll come over for you. And I'll walk down the street by Mag-dal-ene and into the College and I'll say 'Where's this bastard from New Zealand', and I'll take you back where you belong."

I often wish he would come. For I am sure he could stand in the centre of the quad and call, as he calls one of his dogs across a bush valley, and no-one would take any notice except to direct him to my room. And people that met him would like him and would give him beer to drink, would admire him for his strength and good sense, and enjoy his language. And I know also that he would like the men here. "Soft, I reckon," he would say, "not one on'em could milk a cow, I bet," he would add, to assert himself. "But nice fellows, I guess." He would probably talk to them about the Union Jack and the British Empire, which would at least be novel.

I was very grateful to the first man who called to see me at Oxford. He lived on the same staircase and it seemed a neighbourly act. I was unpacking and feeling homesick when he came in and what cheered me apart from his friendliness was that he seemed to be even more melancholy than I was myself. He was attractive and charmingly intelligent but a gentle and Hamlet-like sorrow seemed to brood over him. When we had introduced ourselves and had done with the casualties of formality, he leant against the mantelpiece and talked to me while I tried to arrange books on a very dusty bookshelf.

"I should think this is the worst room in the College," he said, gazing bleakly round him. I had suspected it myself. "But then," he added, "there's little to be said for any of them. Have you met Harry?"

"Yes."

"I should think," he said, with gentle and resigned amusement, "he's the worst scout in College." The general outlook did not seem encouraging.

"But then," he said, "it's getting towards the end of term and I've had toothache all the week, not" he added quickly, "that things are any better at any other time."

"Don't you like Oxford?" I asked him. You see, I had been brought up to believe that young men passed the golden years of their lives at Oxford.

"It's a pretty bloody place," he said morosely. "You see there's nothing to do. The food's bloody too, but you wouldn't mind that if it weren't for the general dullness."

"How do you mean there's nothing to do?" I asked him.

"Well, there isn't really. One day's just like another. You spend your time talking to a lot of men who don't care if they see you or not. And they're all pretty dull. I hope you haven't come here to be amused."

I said that I didn't know really why I had come except for a vague idea of being educated.

"Oh, there's work, of course," he said. "I read the classics myself. Splendid mental exercise for a retired and elderly gentleman I should think, but it seems a little pointless to me at present. This isn't quite the way I should choose to spend the best years of my life. However," he said, more cheerfully, "better than sleeping on the embankment, I suppose. But if you've never done that you don't realise the difference, I suppose, or how well off you are. That's true, isn't it?" He went towards the door. "Hope you'll like it," he said. "Ask me if there's anything I can do. Good night."

That visit really cheered me up a great deal. Generally speaking, people at Oxford did not go out of their way to meet you, and you were grateful when they did. There were, of course, exceptions to this.

When I came to Oxford politics had succeeded religion in the general interest, but the Oxford Group worked on steadily and some of its proselytising was tryingly social. I used to sit next to a member in Hall occasionally, a very nice man who must have been thought little of in the Group because of the polite way in which he refrained from forcing his views upon people. We used to exchange spasmodic remarks in a rather shy way. He came from a provincial University which is often worse than being a Colonial, at Oxford. "Very poor mutton," he would say, and then fearing, quite wrongly, that he had offended me by offering conversation of too low a standard, he would follow it up with, "There's a certain splendour in Ezra Pound's classicism, isn't there?" or something like that. It was all very difficult and we could help each other little. One evening he had a fellow member as his guest, who talked rapidly to both of us and who quickly invited me to coffee in his host's rooms. There was a cloistral silence about the half dozen people who gathered there after dinner, but I recognised one black sheep. He winked encouragingly at me as he took the best arm chair. Conversation was desultory. The man whom I had met at dinner, talked most of the time and annoyed me by asking what part of Australia I came from. After a while, he said suddenly "Shall we have a quiet time?" "It's been fairly quiet so far," murmured the black sheep half to himself; but we had a "quiet time" nevertheless.

The next day I found myself asked to a tea party. There was another stranger in the fold this time, a young man whose fiery socialism was contained with difficulty during the afternoon. The members of the Group do not smoke or drink, but they eat very well. As the shadows deepened, in that quiet hour which succeeds the day, they began to discuss God over the ruins of cream cakes and crumpets. The only explosion came when the "Leader" told us how he had lived, during the last year, "on ten pounds and God;" and the Socialist, who was also an American, and who should really never have been asked, replied, "I guess we have another name for that where I come from."

The process of attempted conversion was not, as a rule, very prolonged. The sinners were dropped by the way. I was left, however, with the unhappy feeling that their converts must often be men who were merely lonely, and were glad to accept the fellowship of "house parties" and "quiet teas".

One was very tenacious of company and friendship in those first few weeks, but after a time it became easy to meet people. You met them all ways, playing games or more casually. One friend led to another. You met men at clubs, or at parties, talked and arranged to meet again, and mutually forgot or remembered. There were Irishmen or Scotchmen or Frenchmen, Americans rich in expressiveness, and Indians feminine of mind. It was difficult to know whether people liked you or not, and if you were wise you did not worry. The principle seemed to be that one returned the hospitality that was given one. If, after that, you were mutually or singly bored, the acquaintance ended.

Sherry parties existed simply for the purpose of bringing people together, not for the sherry. I found the first one I went to a terrifying experience. Over a hundred people were crowded into a room that would have offered comfort to about six. There were drinks at one end of the room, and occasionally someone would appear with a bottle and fill your glass. If no-one appeared, you filled it yourself. There were delicate savouries to eat, and although one rarely saw the guests eating, they would all be gone by the end of the party.

There was no time to be introduced to anybody. My host was swallowed in the throng. The combined sound of so many voices was shattering. But the general result of standing there in that black hole of Calcutta was that you talked to the person nearest to you. I found myself in conversation with a limpid man who elected to talk about the most suitable furnishings for rooms in Oxford.

"I often feel that something sombre, black, perhaps" he said dreamily, "and then my scout comes in, and he has such a very odd face."

Of his scout's peculiar face I heard no more, for somebody joined us with a bottle of sherry and a glass. The dreamy young man took the bottle, filled the three glasses and put the bottle on the windowsill behind him.

"We were talking about furnishing," he said.

"How nice for both of you," said the newcomer, and turning he bored his way through the throng, towards a young woman in a flowered hat. The great hat oscillated deftly as she welcomed him.

"A strange fellow that," said the dreamy man, "tiringly interested in women."

"Most of us are," I ventured, rather bashfully.

"It is possible," he said grandly, "to escape these vices." At this point I began to realise that the greatest necessity at these affairs was a stock of light conversation which would be equally interesting to everybody. The stock opening remarks of "What College are you at?" and "What are you reading?" did not lead one very far, and my education in aesthetics had been sadly neglected.

Fortunately, at that moment, there was a stir beside us. A celebrity had arrived, a handsome man whose every gesture was of studied eloquence. Something of a circle was cleared about him. It seemed that he was an actor, almost one might say, by profession, and he appeared to be describing some recent performance.

"But the production! My dear fellow! As I said to Blake, repertory after all is repertory. However, we did what we could. Did you read the notices?" They had apparently been studied with great care. "It was really very touching, that last night. I did not know what to say. I just came forward and said simply, 'Thank you, thank you'."

The dreamy young man and myself had been listening to this and become part of the group. Conversation in it became more general and it tended to disintegrate. I began to look on myself as lost and also to feel vaguely that I should like to meet the young woman in the flowered hat. She looked simple and kind. I never did meet her and it is very unlikely that she was either of those things. There were about six women in the room, so many centres of attraction in a sea of mankind. It was only at sherry parties that one met women in Oxford. I often thought that invitations should be issued for "Sherry 5.30 – 7" and, in brackets, "there will be so many ladies present".

It was obviously impossible to ask the authority on furnishings to introduce me to the girl in the flowered hat, and in the meantime, I was afraid that he must be finding me very dull. Someone, I saw, had manoeuvred her into a corner beside the table and was free from interruption while he talked to her. I applauded the hand of a social master.

I seemed to have been at the party for a long time. We drank weak sherry assiduously and in time I found myself talking to someone else. "Queer things, sherry parties, aren't they?" he said. I never went to a sherry party without someone commenting on their queerness, or without doing so myself. "The trouble with all these people," another man said, "is that they have no religion. We've got to become God-conscious again." The room became blue with a fog of cigarette smoke, and gradually the room began to empty. It was almost possible to walk across it by now. The women left early, gratified with display and adulation. I found my host, who was seizing the opportunity to fill his own glass. He looked tired and harassed. "I'm so glad you could come," he said when I thanked him, but it seemed doubtful if he would ever have noticed my absence. Outside the air was cool and delightful. I walked down the street with a Canadian who talked about the beauties of Oxford. "It certainly makes my home town look a factory job," he said.

In time I became seasoned to the task. I went to sherry parties armed with conversation which, if not brilliant, was adequate. Never, I fear, did I attain to the practised ease of the accomplished who moved so gracefully from group to group, but two glasses of sherry gave me at least the illusion of social aplomb. And I learned that if I met anyone I liked, I was to say, "Could we perhaps lunch together some day next week?"

If it was a woman, she would probably refer to a notebook, and after finding that she was engaged to lunch every day for two weeks with so many different men, she would agree graciously and charmingly to come at the end of that time, as if it was to be her one pleasure at the conclusion of a wearying social round. Having achieved that, I used to retire to where the sherry was and talk to some disillusioned man. There were always a lot of them. "Disgusting, aren't they?" a man said to me once, "all these parties, with women preening themselves." He drank darkly and referred me to D.H. Lawrence.

It was a life that was mainly conversational and it went on pleasantly enough. We should, perhaps, have tired of it more easily, but it was very entertaining. It is possible to know a great many people casually, and to see them all at one time or another. There were about five thousand men and women at Oxford when I was there. It was possible to know about two hundred men, and perhaps twenty women, if you had a good memory and went out all the time. You could know about thirty men really well and no women, and it was an achievement to know six men intimately.

Long ago, in New Zealand, an Oxford man told me that one went to Oxford to make friends; and I think this is true only there are limitations to be set. It is true that nowhere else is there such ease, so many leisured moments, and nowhere else, I would be inclined to add, people who are so interesting and attractive in a social way. But friendship is a curious thing. To my mind there must be some element of stress which will occasion it, something which gives a use to understanding and intuition and sympathy. In Oxford one is very rarely faced with a serious situation, or indeed with any slight discomfort. Only by living with a man can you understand him. If you live in a good hotel, every luxury is a bar to your appreciation of him. Oxford is only a moderately good hotel but its comforts are enough to satisfy the young: everything there was so easy, life, on its material side so simple, that the emphasis came to be placed only on social qualities.

These qualities are very valuable. They are the good wine of life which is worth drinking, but they need a foundation. Friendship, I believe, is based on a measure of unselfishness; and if it be answered that there is no such thing, I would call it then an imaginative quality of the mind which can understand the wishes of other people, can sympathise with them and help them. A recognition of this imaginative quality seems necessary to friendship. It has been said of the War that it brought out unexpected qualities in men, and this is probably true, although not a justification for the War itself.

It was too easy at Oxford to regard people as a form of entertainment and the emphasis being placed on these social qualities, one came at times to distrust them. It was sometimes difficult to feel that even the men you knew most intimately were your friends.

Perhaps I exaggerate this, or perhaps I lacked intuition enough to accept friendship on trust, and not to need proof of it. Most of the time we were happy and glad enough to amuse each other, but I remember that at times, and towards the end of a term, people became dissatisfied, tired of each other and of themselves.

[I was] at lunch one day with three Englishmen and an American, all of whom I knew well and liked. The spring rain was beating against the window, in that indeterminate time of the year when no season seems to have power over the earth. We talked casually, without much effort. Somebody happened to describe a man whom he had just met as "interesting".

"Hell," said our host, suddenly and surprisingly, "how I hate that word."

"Why, it's common enough in Oxford. It's what we all try to be, God help us."

"It makes me realise how all you want is entertainment and perhaps food when you come to lunch with me."

"Well, the food's all right anyway."

"Thanks, and I suppose I can leave the conversation to you."

We were all embarrassed by his seriousness. It was unnecessary for him to be unhappy, and we all liked him.

"You English," said the American, with a[23] gnomic earnestness that is[24] common to the United States, "are a decadent nation, with too much time for thinking and too little room for action. I include the Colonies and I am happy to assist at this decadence." And having reminded us that the art of living was to avoid thought, he drank deeply of audit ale.

I can remember a number of conversations that began like that and ended as lightly, and I do not know now what moral is to be drawn.

Day by Day

I want by writing to break some of the incoherence that life at Oxford had for me. The strangeness of arrival had dissipated any false[25] dreams I had, and then for a while the reality of each experience gave everything emphasis. But that, too, passed and I know that I was living there without observing men or events. It was a different life to anything I had experienced before, and yet very easy and natural. I am left really with only an impression of having been to Oxford and with the memory of confused and disconnected incidents in a context which I find it hard to describe. It was, as I have said, the absence of any ordering compulsion that made it like this. I knew some men who were close students and made their lives round that, with everything else as a recreation, but they were few in number and most men followed a less harmonious way.

I read in a guidebook before I came, a description of a day in Oxford. It was factually true but it seems a long way from reality. Thinking of this one evening, I asked a man if he could describe his day to me.

"Yes," he said, "but this has been a rather curious day."

"More so than yesterday?"

"Why, no," and he thought for a while. "I think," he said, "I see every day as more or less the same, but with something unusual in it. I know it is that that leaves me with the impression of Oxford as of a very odd place."

When we had talked for an hour, we found that we could reconstruct his day. His talking made a selection which I would have found difficult myself, and it gives me some of the reality which I need to remember.

His scout, he said, called him at ten minutes to eight coming in noisily with a tin of shaving water. "Ten minutes to eight, sir," he said. His scout was a merry little man called Bert with whom he was very friendly. He did not say anything but lay half awake, heavily drowsy as he always was in the mornings. He knew that he should get up and go to roll-call. Half-consciously he felt all that it would mean, dressing and going out into the cold, and then perhaps, waiting for a bath. He tried to remember how many roll-calls he had done in the term and felt sleepily angry. While he considered all this, the clock began to chime the hour. There was still time if he hurried. He turned over and went to sleep again.

Bert called him again at half past eight. "Your breakfast's getting cold, sir," he said. This was an old and favourite joke. His breakfast consisted of cornflakes with milk and tea which he made himself. He woke up now and lay listening. He could hear Bert going to the room above him, walking heavily because he had been wounded in the War and was still lame. Then he got up and found his slippers and dressing gown. The sitting room was bitterly cold and outside there were traces of fog, clearing on to a grey sky. His shaving water had grown cold and he studied his face in the mirror to see whether he need shave.

"Hell," he thought, "who cares?" and he took up his towel and went out towards the bathrooms. He had to cross two quads but most people were breakfasting and he met only one man with whom he exchanged a jaundiced greeting. One advantage of getting up at this time was that the baths were empty. He lay in a hot bath and thought about the work that he should do. He was in his third year and reading "Greats" without enthusiasm, but he had a theory that if you thought about your work long enough, you approached it with pleasure.

It was ten to nine when he got back to his room. He put an electric kettle on to boil while he dressed. There was a letter on the table for him and he took it into the bedroom to read. It was from a girl who was supposed to be coming to tea with him that day.

"Dear Eric," she wrote, "About tea this afternoon – do you mind if I bring someone with me? You said nothing about it on Monday and I forgot to ask you. You know it is a rule that I don't like breaking, or perhaps you have asked someone else? Of course I know you will say that I came to lunch with Kenneth by myself, but there really was nearly some trouble over that. So I will bring Joan whom you have met unless I hear to the contrary. Yours, Dorothy."

"Christ," he said, half aloud, when he read this. "Does she think I'm Casanova? And if she did she'd be flattering herself. What a place!" and he thought savagely about Oxford and the silliness of its women. For a moment he thought about another[26] girl whom he liked[27] and who lived in London, and he realised that he didn't really care whether Dorothy came to tea or not. At that point his kettle boiled over on the floor and he cursed again as he turned it off and made the tea. But when he had eaten something and had drunk three cups of tea, he felt better. He sat in front of the fire and smoked a cigarette. Then he went to see Kenneth who had started work for the day but did not mind being interrupted.

"Look here," he said, "what about this woman Dorothy?" and showed him the letter. Kenneth laughed.

"I never heard her mention chaperones before," he said. "You must have a reputation."

"Why these women can't show a little sense, I don't know," he said. "Does she think she'll be assaulted? I'm damned if I'll have Joan to tea." He borrowed a sheet of notepaper and wrote:

"Dear Dorothy, I would rather you came to tea by yourself. If you would prefer it, we can have tea somewhere in town. I shall expect you about 4.30. Yours, Eric."

He left Kenneth and posted the letter in the lodge, and with the satisfactory feeling of having asserted himself, he went back to his room. Bert was just clearing away the breakfast. He said nothing to him because he did not want to be drawn into a long conversation which would be difficult to end. He gathered some books together and began to write an essay on the Battle of Marathon which was due to be handed in at nine o'clock the next morning. It took him nearly half an hour to write the first paragraph and then he saw that most of it could be taken from the *Cambridge Ancient History*. But first he went to a friend on the next staircase who had done the same essay a week before.

"Is there anything I ought to read on this?" he asked. His friend gave him his own essay with some notes. "There's a paper in the *Classical Review* that I should have looked at," he said.

"That'll be impressive," said Eric and thanked him.

"Are you going to Carritt's lecture?" his friend asked him.

"No," he said, "I haven't got time," and he took the essay and notes down to the College library and found the paper in the *Classical Review*. While he made notes from it he exchanged remarks with a man who was copying an essay from the *Cambridge History of English Literature*.

"You should have read English," this man said. "It's a more gentlemanly life."

After that, he went back to his rooms and by twelve o'clock he had done two pages of his essay. He took a cigarette and went down to the lodge to see if there were any letters. There was a bill and a letter from his father. He put them both in his pocket, and thought ironically that he could answer his father's letter adequately by re-directing the bill to him. He went along to the Junior Common Room which was almost deserted, and he sat by the fire there for ten minutes, while he read a special article in the *News Chronicle* and the reviews in the *New Statesman*. Fortified with this resume of modern affairs, he went back to his room and continued[28] his description of the Battle of Marathon.

By a quarter to one, he was tired of it and wanted to talk to someone. Also he felt ready for lunch. There was more life in the stairway and in the quad, with men returning from lectures and leaving their work, and it made him feel restless. He went into [a] room on the stairway opposite to him, where a friend lived. When Bert came up they told him to set their lunch together, and while they ate cold meat and salad, they talked in a desultory way, mainly about the characteristics of their mutual friends. After lunch someone else came in and, in a sleepy way, they talked on. He could not remember much of what they talked about except that Aldous Huxley came into it.

Then he remembered that he was down to play football and went out to the notice-board in the lodge to see if the game was still on. It was and so he came back and changed and then walked up to the ground. The game itself was rather fragmentary, like most College matches. He did not really enjoy football but played the game out of a sense of duty and for exercise. They had to wait ten minutes for a referee, while he got cold, and when they started he was hit on the head in a line-out which dispirited him instead of making him angry. They were beaten 10-3. But he felt fine afterwards, walking back tired and muddy, and then having a bath. Also he was looking forward to Dorothy's arrival and considering what he should say to her. By the time he had dressed he had ten minutes to spare, which he filled in by setting the tea-cups ready. He prepared only for two and put the sofa in front of the fire so that they would both have to sit on it. Hot-buttered toast arrived from the buttery and finally Dorothy came herself at about twenty to five.

He welcomed her with a well-prepared ease of manner. "Where do you want to have tea?" he asked her.

She smiled, slightly embarrassed. "I think I can stay here," she said. "I had to be very rude to Joan. You must ask her to tea some day, and I don't really like breaking rules like this."

"I don't think any rules are worth keeping with which you can't agree," he said – rather sententiously, but it impressed her. By the time they had discussed their attitude to the regulations of Oxford, he had managed to make the tea. He sat beside her on the sofa, and being hungry, ate twice as much as she would permit herself. She seemed to him rather more attractive than when he had first met her and he thought that he liked her. But after the conversation had wandered for a while, she insisted on talking seriously about religion. It appeared that her father was a Church of England minister and she could not satisfy her conscience about attending services or being confirmed. He was not at all interested but made satisfactory comments without really advancing any opinion. He believed personally that all churches were obstacles to social progress and should be abolished. He found himself irritated by the consciously correct way in which she sat and spoke. "Damn you," he thought. "You don't really know anything and you won't learn." At a quarter to six, she rose to go. "It's been frightfully nice," she said. He did not know whether she had enjoyed herself or not, whether he wanted her to come again or not, whether he liked her or she liked him. "I hope you'll come again," he said as he helped her on with her coat. They walked down into the High together and then she caught a bus and he came back to College. He felt as if he had been wasting his time. "They're inhuman," he said to himself, "You never get to know them. Another indeterminate, frustrated afternoon."

It was dark now as he came back into his own quad. He met two men whom he knew slightly, coming down the stairs just outside his room. 'We've been putting Johnson to bed," they told him. "He's very drunk." He felt sorry for Johnson whom he liked better than either of these two[29] men and he went up to his room. Johnson was a man with a lot of money who entertained a great deal, but he had always had the impression that he was rather unhappy and he felt friendly towards him. He was lying now on a sofa, covered with a rug, his face very pale. He opened his eyes when the other came in.

"Can I do anything for you?" he asked him.

Johnson smiled wanly. "I wish you'd get me a drink of

water," he said. He found some water in the bedroom and gave it to him. Johnson sat up and drank it.

"I've been a damn fool," he said. "I was drinking brandy after lunch and like a fool I wouldn't stay inside. Got progged and had to be brought here."

He did not know what to say to him. He knew that he would probably be sent down at least for the term, because he had been in trouble before.[30]

"It's a bloody nuisance," Johnson said. "My father doesn't know I drink. There'll be hell to pay." He closed his eyes again.

"Nothing else I can do?"

"No. Thanks for coming up. I'm going to sleep."

Back in his room again, he had forgotten about Dorothy and was vaguely worried, thinking of Johnson. He guessed that his friends cared little for him, and that he lived this way[31] because he was unhappy and to replace a lot of things. But after a while he cleared the table and returned to his essay. At half past six Bert came in again to clear the tea things.

"Don't disturb Mr Johnson, Bert," he said to him. "He's sleeping."

"All right, sir." Bert gathered the cups onto a tray.

"Young lady to tea today sir?" he said. He was very interested in the affairs of the men whom he looked after.

"Yes, Bert," he said, laughing.

"Always know when it's just tea for two with you, sir. Was it the young lady with dark hair?"

"No, another one. You haven't seen this one."

"Ah, I liked the little dark lady, sir. She'd make a good wife."

Eric laughed again; he was always cheered by talking to Bert. "How do you know?" he said.

"I've got a good wife myself, sir, that I have."

"But did you know a lot of other girls as well? It's not much use otherwise."

Bert enjoyed that too. "Plenty," he said, and went out laughing, as one man to another, having enjoyed a man's joke.

Eric returned to his books. The Battle of Marathon was vaguely interesting him but he disliked the actual labour of writing about it. "I could make a good story of this," he thought, "only it would be wasted," and he continued to precis the *Cambridge History*, adding touches of his own which he considered tended to realism. He heard the clock in the tower strike seven and then the bell ring for chapel, but he was so used to these things that they meant no more to him than time past. When the clock struck the half hour and the bell rang again for Hall, he took his gown and went quickly down to dinner.

He had sat with the same men in Hall now for nearly two years, and they did not bother much to entertain one another,[32] but there was a guest there who slightly broke the ordinariness of it all and made the conversation more general. But they talked first about Johnson, being all interested in College scandal, however slight, and for the rest mainly about work and lectures. Someone as usual, maligned the food, but he had heard the same man complain of the way the College roasted potatoes so often, that he had come to look on the remark as almost part of the potatoes which were, indeed, always the same.

After Hall, he went to coffee in a friend's rooms. There were five people there who usually met at that time of the day. He could not remember much of what they talked about, except that one man was describing chapel service in the morning at which he had read the lesson.

"It's hell," he said, "only the chaplain and me. I never know when to stand up and as for responses, I'm a lost soul."

"Weren't you educated in the Church of England, you pagan?"

"Not me. Useful for jobs though – I often wish I had been."

"Well, did you find the lesson all right – that's all that matters?"

"Yes, only I read the whole chapter by mistake instead of the first sixteen verses."

"What was it?"

"Something out of Corinthians, couldn't understand it, needs a context I suppose."

They played a gramophone and he smoked a second cigarette. Conversation went on through it. Kenneth was there and wanted to know about Dorothy, but he resolved to be uncommunicative, except to say that she had come by herself after all. Kenneth was very amused by it all, just the same.

"Is she coming again?" he asked.

"I don't know," said Eric, "nor whether I want her to."

At nine they all went to their rooms to work. Nobody interrupted him and by eleven he had finished his essay. The last page gave him some trouble, because it involved a summary and a few conclusions. But he finished it and felt satisfied; and then he came to talk to me.

"It's a fair summary," he said when he had finished. "Some days are clearer but not many. When I first came up I used to do more. Sit up all night talking about God and politics. I don't want to now. I know a few people well and what's worse I know everything they will say. When I meet new people I make more effort. We all do. But I guess the rest is just living."

It was half past twelve when we finished talking and went to bed. I do not know what he thought about before he went to sleep.

Rustic Witness

An Interlude[33]

January, and still it is winter with us. The beasts stand patiently in the fields. Winter is something to be endured, something very old and wearying. "June in January" the gramophones are playing, but still the rain falls and cold binds the earth.[34] And then one morning, snow on the dark roofs – it is winter's charity.

But soon comes February and another year to the children of men. There are crocuses in the gardens and on St. Valentine's day, the birds sing merrily in the parks. Looking down on Oxford one day from the hills at Beckley, I watched a cold wind driving clouds across the midland plains with bursts of hail. But for a moment the clouds lifted and Oxford lightened in the valley below.

The March winds and more flowers, some leaves and blossoms on the trees. When there was sun and lambs upon the downs, I went to Sussex.[35] That must have been a fine county once, but now something has commercialised it. They had even called the fine inn where we stayed, "Ye Olde Tudor Inne," and put an antique shop opposite it. There was better beer and fewer visitors at the Victorian drinking house down the road, but even there I met a pseudo-rustic who talked as if he had read Hardy. "There be rabbits here, that there be," he would say, or "Old Tom Benn wot ploughed that field, he never smiled again arter his daughter died," but nobody paid much attention to him. Most of the fellows who came in there were good men. They didn't fit into the pattern, but the countryside had lost its pattern. They were half way to being townsmen with tastes still for simple things, like horse-racing and football; they were very like men I had known in my own country on the outskirts of small towns.

But I found something of an older England, more striking, more inexplicable, coming homewards in the country between London and Oxford.[36] There is a small inn somewhere there.[37] I cannot believe that it has a flourishing trade for it is a long way from main roads on a country lane running between wooded hills, and it is set back even from that[38] lane so that it has all the appearance of a farm-house. Larches grow in front of it and there are a lot of[39] flowers in the garden.[40]

The room into which we were shown was like many of its kind,[41] only smaller and more homely. There were two dark heavy tables and long benches laid beside them. The walls were stained dark – not with the finished antiquity that one learns to associate with show-places,[42] but more simply, as if by the hand of the amateur. There were three old prints on the walls; they were not[43] Alken prints, but such as Alken might have done, queer hunting pictures of strange whiskered men and titles beneath them that were doubtless funny once but now seem only sad.[44] And there was a fire-place, large, bricked and open, with crouching chimney seats and a crumbling log fire.

He was sitting in the far corner of the room beside a table when we came in and he nodded to us. There were three or four other men in the room whom I cannot call to mind but I remember him particularly and what he looked like. Yet he was not strange or remarkable in any way but such a man as one sees often throughout some parts of[45] the country. He was a big man and broad-shouldered but past his youth. He had come there[46] from his work, with worn coat and corduroy trousers and the clay still clinging to his boots. His face was red with a deep sunny glow, the skin roughened by wind and weather but[47] curiously fresh, and he had a moustache grizzled and drooping, like Bairnsfather's "old contemptibles" who were loved in War.[48] He sat there with one huge hand laid on the table beside a grey pewter mug of ale and a massive square of bread, the other on his knee and he bent forward slightly as he sat, not in contemplation of anything but strangely unregardful.[49] He ate and drank slowly and very carefully, with long pauses[50] in between, and yet he must have been hungry for this was the end of a day's work.[51] But[52] his whole attitude was of one who would not be hurried into action but would move slowly to his end.

We sat down with him and talked to him, but there was a long silence first, felt as a prelude of calm to the rare luxury of conversation. He did not talk himself but answered our questions and added remarks very slowly and seriously, speaking in a quiet, deep South country voice that rose and fell on the words. He told us that it would not rain on the morrow: the small flecked clouds we had seen at sunset meant a north wind which would bring no [rain][53] but it would be cold, very cold. My companion murmured something about the wireless weather report, but he only smiled.[54] From that[55] we turned to farming and the land about there. No, he knew little of sheep or cows – he could kill and dress a sheep (smiling). There had been sheep run there once but it was a long time ago and the land had been cut up since then. He worked on the land – not his own land but[56] another man's farm – but he had a small allotment of village land[57] where he grew vegetables.

At this point there was an interruption. "Tell 'n about they turnips o' yourn," somebody called out, but he would not tell us, and finally his friends gave us the story. It was a long and complicated account of how some other man won a prize at the show with turnips which he had taken from our friend's allotment, and it wound up to a climax in which both men had stood looking at the turnips, afraid to say what was in their minds, and then one had said, "Ah, they be fine turnips," and the other had added grimly, "Ah, and well grown and all," and that was the end of the story. And then, I was distracted for a moment by a little man who told us how he could put[58] twenty cigarettes into a packet made for ten; and when I turned round again they were talking about trees.[59] Trees were his great affection. He had been grafting fruit trees earlier in the day. Yes, he did a lot of grafting, he did nearly all the grafting in the district, had done for many years. He could make pippins grow upon crab apples.

Then another pause, while he finished his bread and leaned forward with the pewter mug between his hands, smiling non-committally at a remark that was thrown to him from the other table. We took up the tale again. He did not seem to mind our questioning but answered always with a[60] slow and deliberate courtesy. Had he lived long in the village? Yes, all his life and had been away little, except for the war. Yes, he had served in the war, in the county regiment: he had been in France from 1915 onwards. My friend, who had also seen war service, asked him of places and battles. He had been in the beginning of the Somme, and again at Passchendaele. There was nothing more to say. He had been in the trenches, had probably killed men, had been in long danger of life, and had suffered and endured but there was nothing to say. He had accepted it as he accepted[61] life, as something to be lived through quietly and effectively.

And I knew then in what way his strength made him different from other men I had known. I remembered talking about the war to farmers in my own country, men of the land whom I always felt to have wisdom and knowledge. And one man in particular, I remember talking with, while we waited in a valley for some sheep that were being moved down from the hills. "Do you think there'll be war again?" I asked him, for there was talk of it at the time. And the question seemed to upset him, because he did not answer for a while, and then he said, half to himself, "It'd make you think, but the two men who cleared this valley – and it was high bush too – were killed in the last war." And again, after a pause, "I reckon there'll be no war. There's no call to go across the seas to fight these days," and we did not speak about it again.

For you see, these men did not[62] see themselves as part of a system, and they had not[63] been born to accept the world. They had their own fight, which was with the rimu and the rata and the matai, and then with the fern and bracken that came after it. Their one destiny was the market price that gave them success or failure and they did not always bow to that. It is[64] only in the new countries that you can live like that and the chance[65] may go from there in time. It seemed the only way of living to me then, but I am not sure that it is the happiest. It was before my time, but there was another man in that same valley who came back from the war with one arm. He found like many others that his half-cleared farm had been left to go back, for though they worked as hard as they could to sell butter at half a crown a pound, they couldn't hold all the land when the men were away. For a while he had a man to help him and then the war prices died over night and he knew that the farm could not[66] be made to pay. They say that he used just to wander round the farm with a gun under his one arm, shooting at rabbits and then one day he shot himself. There were[67] a lot like that, men[68] who came back from the war and, with four years gone, were beaten and broken by the older war with the land. I know why they would question it, if the bugles went again to-day. These are the back-block men of whom I speak, and they make their own lives.

And now I was talking to a farmer in Buckinghamshire a world away, and I could honour his strength. In a sense he had endured more successfully than these other men. I suppose that he was of[69] "the people of England that never have spoken yet".[70] There cannot be many of them left.[71] Each day more and more are caught up into a life that necessitates the subtleties of modern civilisation, so that they lose their aloofness and become part of a living and striving state. They become sharpened to observe, and to fear.

But[72] this man was of a different order, almost of a different world. He did not live in the oblivion of a peasant class, passing through life like the cattle of the fields. There was a richness in his eyes and an intelligence in the quiet restraint of his voice. He was aloof and apart in a curious and impregnable way.[73] He had not made the world into which he had been born nor did he desire to alter it. He had accepted what men had imposed upon him, a place in society and long labour; a cruel war – to him unnecessary, probably much suffering; never the sharpness of actual poverty but always the hardships of pressing needs, without remission. He had accepted all this and had been untouched by it, and would go on, perhaps unconsciously a little scornful of the world about him. He would be[74] always dominant and undefeatable.

It was almost closing time by now. He rose first and nodded good night to us and to the rest of the company, stretching his fine figure, and went out, stooping to pass the low lintel of the doorway. The door shut behind him and we could hear his hob-nailed footsteps going down the paved path between the larches in the garden. And we had time for another drink while we thought about him.[75]

Textual Notes

1 Both the quotations are taken from Chaucer's *Parlement of Foules*, lines 127-30.
2 In this and the following chapter, Mulgan includes a number of allusions to contemporary songs from the First World War. "Good-bye-ee" was a popular wartime song, c. 1915, by R. P. Weston and Bert Lee.
3 "Absence makes the heart grow fonder (for somebody else)" was written by Samuel Warren and Joseph Young (1929); "Poor me, poor you" by Ray Noble around 1933.
4. called the tui] written above line.
5. Mulgan may have encountered the unusual phrase "bent world" in the recently-published second edition of Gerard Manley Hopkins' poems, where it occurs in "God's Grandeur". As he notes in a letter of April, 1935, Sisam had been encouraging him to go on to do a thesis on Bridges and Hopkins (*A Good Mail* p. 74).
6. think] written above line; originally read "wonder".
7. The typescript originally continued "and calling loudly for whiskies", but the words have been deleted.
8. These lyrics (the line should read "weep no more today") occur in Stephen Foster's minstrel song, "My Old Kentucky Home".
9. vigorously] written above line; originally read "deeply".
10. long] added above line.
11. There is an Irish love song called simply "Tipperary", but given the general content of the other songs mentioned here, this is more likely to refer to the better known "It's a long way to Tipperary" (1912) by Jack Judge, which was sometimes used as a marching song; "Keep the home fires burning" was a patriotic song from 1914 written by Ivor Novello; "There's a long, long trail a-winding" was another popular song from the war, written by Stoddard King and Alonzo Elliott around 1913-14.
12. The origins of the Londonderry air are still a matter of some dispute. Interestingly, the air is often associated with Limavady, where Mulgan was briefly stationed during his posting to Northern Ireland.
13. The poem, first published in 1738, is simply entitled "London: a Poem"; its subtitle "In Imitation of the Third Satire of Juvenal" indicates the justice of

Mulgan's comment. The second comment is found in Boswell's *Life* as an entry in the record of 1777. Boswell had wondered whether, if he were to move to London, he might grow tired of it, to which Johnson had replied with the well-known rejoinder that Mulgan cites here.

14. "While I breathe, I hope." Popularly attributed to Cicero.
15. advertisements] originally read "bills".
16. Mulgan seems to be conflating two of Pope's Letters: one, to Martha Blount, provides a description such as he suggests here, of approaching Oxford by horseback at evening, and being struck by its unique atmosphere. Pope also wrote a Letter to the Earl of Burlington which provides an account of a journey to Oxford "with Bernard Lintot, a Bookseller", but it contains no observations about the journey itself; indeed, Lintot's ceaseless conversation (as Pope remarked) left little opportunity for observation. Lintot, incidentally, was a noted rival of Tonson, with whom Mulgan confuses him.
17. Brasenose College.
18. From "The Dying Patriot", a poem by James Elroy Flecker.
19. The usual formula for matriculation begins "Quo die comparuit coram me..." (on this day appeared before me ...).
20. Mulgan is drawing on an incident recorded in Boswell's *Life of Johnson*, in which Johnson made the following observation about his Pembroke tutor: He was a very worthy man, but a heavy man, and I did not profit much by his instructions. Indeed, I did not attend him much. The first day after I came to college, I waited upon him, and then staid away four. On the sixth, Mr. Jorden asked me why I had not attended. I answered, I had been sliding [that is, skating] in Christ Church meadow.
21. as a pastime for] written above the line.
22. Mulgan is referring to Auckland University College, not University College, Oxford.
23. a] added above line; originally read "the".
24. that is] added above line.
25. false] added above line.
26. another] added above line; originally read "the".
27. whom he liked] originally read "whom he thought he liked".
28. continued] added above line; originally read "went on with".
29. two] added above line; originally read "three".
30. The terms "progged" and "sent down" both relate to internal disciplinary processes within the University. To be "progged" (more formally to be "proctorized") is to be arrested, reprimanded or disciplined by a University proctor. Students who were "sent down" were removed from the University, temporarily or permanently.
31. this way] added above line; originally read "a fast life".
32. one another] added above line; originally read "each other".
33. An Interlude] RW2 is subtitled "A Study in English Life – By John Mulgan".

34. The imagery here is strongly reminiscent of the Old English poems "The Wanderer" and "The Seafarer", which both speak of hail binding the earth.
35. Mulgan writes in similar fashion, including mention of "Ye Olde Tudor Inne", in a letter to his parents from Alfriston, Sussex, in May, 1934.
36. RW2 omits all the preceding material.
37. small inn somewhere there] RW2 reads "small inn that stands in the country between London and Oxford."
38. that] RW2 has "that" crossed through, with "the" added above the line.
39. a lot of] RW2 has "many".
40. The incident on which this story is based seems to have taken place in Meadle, Princes Risborough, Buckinghamshire, and the friend who accompanied Mulgan was probably Hector MacQuarrie. Their visit to the pub in Meadle took place very shortly after Mulgan's holiday in Alfriston. See *Long Journey to the Border* pp. 109-10.
41. of its kind] RW2 has "such".
42. show-places] RW2 has "Tudor show-places".
43. walls; they were not] RW2 has "walls – not".
44. Alken] RW2 has "Alden". Henry Alken was a very well-known painter and engraver of the early 19th century, who was particularly famous for his impressions of English sporting life.
45. some parts of] omitted from RW2.
46. come there] RW2 has "come in there".
47. but] RW2 has "yet".
48. like Bairnsfather's ... in War] RW2 has "like the old Bairnsfather 'contemptible' whom we used to love in the war". Bruce Bairnsfather was a very popular cartoonist who flourished in the first half of the 20th century. He was especially famous for the creation of the character "Old Bill". The term "old contemptible" was adopted in self-deprecating fashion by British regular army troops in 1914.
49. This neologism occurs in both versions.
50. drank slowly and very carefully, with long pauses] RW2 has "drank but slowly, very carefully and with long pauses".
51. hungry for this was the end of a day's work] RW2 has " hungry for he had come in there from the fields and this was his supper".
52. But] omitted from RW2.
53. rain] both typescripts have "wind".
54. My companion ... only smiled] omitted from RW2.
55. that] RW2 has "there".
56. but] RW2 has "but on".
57. land] RW2 has "ground".
58. put] added above line.
59. At this point ... talking about trees] omitted from RW2.
60. a] omitted from RW2.

61. accepted] RW2 has "had accepted".
62. did not] added above line; originally read "didn't".
63. had not] added above line; originally read "hadn't".
64. It is] written above line; originally read "It's usually". Not in RW2.
65. the chance] written above line; originally read "it". Not in RW2.
66. could not] added above line; originally read "couldn't".
67. were] added above line; originally read "was".
68. men] added above line; originally read "There are some".
69. And I knew … suppose that he was of] omitted from RW2, which instead has a modified version of the final paragraph: "He rose and nodded good night to us and to the rest of the company, stretching his fine figure, and went out stooping to pass the low lintel of the doorway. The door shut behind him and one could hear his hobnailed footsteps going down the paved path that led through the garden." The sentence that follows begins "These are the people …".
70. The line comes from "The Secret People", a poem by G. K. Chesterton.
71. There cannot be many of them left] RW2 has "There are not many of them".
72. But] omitted from RW2.
73. RW2 has additional sentence here: "I do not believe that anything of ours could touch him or hurt him."
74. He would be] RW2 has "but".
75. It was almost … thought about him] RW2 has " 'For these are the people of England that never have spoken yet'. They are perhaps a dying race, and will pass away from us – or perhaps, as Chesterton has said, they will yet rise and will speak to us. In the meantime, they are still undefeatable."